A Belly Full of Laughs

by

Paul W. Tastad

D1714635

DORRANCE PUBLISHING CO

EST. 1920

PITTSBURGH, PENNSYLVANIA 15238

Dorrance Publishing Co
585 Alpha Drive
Suite 103
Pittsburgh, PA 15238
Visit our website at *www.dorrancebookstore.com*

ISBN: 978-1-4809-1233-5
eISBN: 978-1-4809-1555-8

Special Thanks

To God, for inspiring the jokes.

To people at the gym who patiently listen to my jokes and stories.

And to my wife, for listening to my ideas
and helping me make this book a reality.

Animals

Homes of animals, fish, and insects
They live with royalty: bees.
Their homes are named after our first settlement: ant colonies.
They are learning in their home school of fish.
The messiest room in the house is a pig sty.
The room bears like the best is the den.
Their home stops the water, beaver dam.
A bunch of women making noises is a hen house.
Where you go when you retire: out to pasture
Where you go when you're in trouble with your wife: the doghouse

How We Handle Problems
We milk it for all it's worth: cow.
We get angry and roar like a lion.
We go back to our den and sleep like a bear.
We get sly about it and try to get out of it like a fox.
We hop around the real problem like a bunny.
We try to weasel our way out of it.
We act like a goat and say, "But it wasn't my fault."
We act like a sheep and say, "Everyone is doing it."
We raise a stink about it like a skunk.
We stick our head in the sand like an ostrich.
We badger others with our problems.

Up North the deer are smart; they can even read.
When a sign says "Deer crossing," they wait there to
cross the road.

The Bear Family
His wife's name is Honey.
The husband's name is Teddy.
He likes to give big bear hugs.
He has a grizzly beard.
He likes to hibernate in his man cave.
He growls at anyone who speaks to him.
He likes to wrap up in a bear rug.
You can guess what he sleeps in.
We bearly see him.
He can be so embarrassing.
He wants bear claws for breakfast.
We have to feed him berries for lunch.

Rabbit Family
The father's name is Bugs.
The mother's name is Bunny.

Brer Rabbit, the grandfather, lives with them.
They live in a hole in one.
They have lots of kids, more every year.
Their favorite game is hopscotch.
They listen to hip-hop music.
Their favorite meal is a lettuce salad, cabbage soup, and carrot cake.

Bugs is great in business.
His nose twitches if he smells something wrong
with the deal.
With his big ears, he hears everything that goes on.
He is so loveable, people want to hug him.
His laugh is funny when he goes "Hare, hare."
Instead of giving his hand in a deal, he offers his
foot because everyone knows a rabbit's foot
means good luck.

Bats don't have to fly around to get where they are going; they just drive their Batmobile.

One cousin told the other cousin she swims with sharks. She works at Sea World. The other cousin said, "That is nothing." She works with sharks. She works at a loan office.

A man says his wife reminds him of an old horse because they are both nags.

A politician at a town hall meeting:
He asked for questions.
They started to badger him.
Someone yelled, "Don't try to weasel out of it."
Your last answer stank worse than a skunk.
You act like a snake in the grass.
They were being so baad.
I had a crane in my neck from turning around so much.
I started to get a whooping cough.
I felt like a mad cow.
I had to duck some questions.
I had to bark some answers, and I started to growl at them like a dog.
My voice became horse.
I felt like a fish out of water that went directly into the frying pan.

Music group at an animal clinic:
The group was called the "Three Dog Night."
They were the cat's meow.
The lead singer sang like a canary.
Woody, the piano player, pecked away at the keys.
Pete, the coyote, could yowl and hit those high notes.
They would sing until they all became horse.
To show their appreciation, the crowd would cheer, "Moo, moo."

Cats and Dogs
What we learn from cats and dogs:
When cats get positive strokes and are petted, they purr. That is like saying to us, "Thank you," and they receive the positive strokes.
When dogs get negative strokes, it is like us when someone says something negative to us. We need to do what dogs do and shake it off.

I had to take my dog to the eye doctor. His being a watch dog, it is hard on his eyes.

My wife says I have been acting like a dog lately. When I go to the bathroom and miss the toilet, she says I am marking my territory.

My wife acts like a dog.
She is always hounding me.
She barks at me.
She growls at me when I don't get it right.
She is always picking a bone with me.
I have to fetch for her.
She always wants to go out.
She whines when she doesn't get her way.
She says I am going to the dogs.
She calls me her old hound dog.
I am often in the doghouse.

My wife is like a cat.
She is curious and has to know everything.
She is a copycat.
She takes cat naps when I am talking to her.
She hisses at me when she is upset.
She is always playing with her computer mouse.
She is catty with people.
When she is in cat fight, the fur really flies.

My boss treats me like a dog.
He is always barking orders at me like "Sit,"
"Stay," and "Do this."
When I don't do it right, he growls at me.
He says I am always barking up the wrong tree.
When I am doing nothing, he says I need to quit chasing my tail and get busy.
When I want something from him, he only says that he will give the dog a bone.
I get dog tired.
He says if I don't shape up, I will have to go back to the dog pound,
which is the unemployment office.
He said he wants me to take an obedience class, but it is hard to
teach an old dog new tricks.
If I don't change, I will be dog gone.

What a "ruff-ruff" life.

A man said his dog is so smart, he can even talk. He comes to the man and the man asks the dog what kind of night he had. The dog barks, "Rough, rough." The other man says, "That is nothing." He said his pet duck saved him thousands of dollars. He had a roofing contractor over and they were going over figures when someone let the duck in. The duck goes, "Quack, quack."

A dog writing a letter and saying "Let's be friends":

I know you have a bone to pick with me.
I know you think I have gone to the dogs.
If I am in a conflict, I don't usually growl but turn tail and run.
If I should bite, I am caught up on my shots.
I know you think when I take a bath and am groomed that I am
putting on the dog, but really it is just being me.
I would like to offer you my paw in friendship.
I don't know what else to say but "Woof, woof."

At work, people are like dogs.
The top dog is the boss.
I am the underdog way under the boss.
Sam is the wonder dog; everyone wonders how he got the job.
Joe is a pit bull; when he gets angry, watch out.
Steve is a bull dog; very bullheaded.
Maloney is an Irish setter who just sits around.
John is a pointer, always pointing out our mistakes.
Ray is our wiener dog, always running for office.
John is just an old hound dog, howling all the time about something.
Pedro is our small mailman who nips at our heels like a Chihuahua.
We have a guide dog for the blind and those who don't know what
they are doing, and around here that includes most of us.
When work gets over, we all run out and everyone yells, "Who let the dogs out?"

My friends got their pets during a storm. It was raining cats and dogs.

A man went to a house and a dog came out and bit him. The owner said that his bite was worse than his bark.

A trainer was having her client walk like a dog. I told her she should get her own dog and not make him her pet. I said, "How did you get him to walk like that?" She said she threatened to send him to the pound. I said, "You shouldn't treat him like that." She said next week she was going to teach him how to fetch.

My relatives went to see the play "Cats" but didn't understand it; they are dog people.

A dog is a wonderful companion. When you come home, they jump all over and are excited to see you, while your teenagers barely talk to you. Feed a dog and scratch his belly, and you have a friend for life. Feed your teenagers, it's a different story. "What's this, again? I don't like this. I already ate," and I am not going to tell you what happens when you try to scratch their belly.

Banks

Sayings for a bank:
You can bank on us.
We're rolling in the dough.
We do drive-bys.
We have a payback time.
Our only interest is in your money.
Honest John goes to make a deposit instead of
robbing the bank.
"My Life behind Bars," the dramatic story of a
bank teller
It's not our fault; it's default.

I have a compliant to make about the banks. The money I get from them doesn't
last; it is like throwing money out the window.

I went to the bank to cash my check for three hundred
dollars. The teller counted out the twenties and fifties,
and then she said that I didn't have any sense. I said I
didn't need to go the bank to be insulted; I could get that
at home.

Banker tells his family:
Always save for a rainy day.
He gives his children loans at twenty percent.
His favorite game is Monopoly.
He has the deeds to your future.
His favorite address is Park Place or the Boardwalk.
He thinks all of the holidays are for him, in that they are
called banker's holidays.
He is well bonded with his children and puts lots of stock
in their future.

My aunt works as a teller in a bank. It was a busy Friday
afternoon. A young man with his cap pulled down where
it almost covered his eyes came up to her and handed
her a note. She said, "What is this?" as she looked over

the note. "This is worse than chicken scratch; I can't read this. Tell me what you want." He said in a low voice, "This is a robbery." "Speak up, son, I can't hear you." He says louder, "This is a robbery." "Is it a joint robbery, or are you alone? If you are with someone, you need to point him out." He looked over toward another guy and pointed at him. Now she said, "I have to know this is for real. Show me the weapon." He put a gun on the counter. She picked it up, looked at it, and said, "My grandson has guns that look more real than this." She opened it up. "Yep, I see you got bullets. It looks like everything is in order. Oh, my, look at the time. I am way past my lunch break time. Sorry, I am closed. You will need to go to another teller."

Birds and Eggs

Joining a company:
This is the secretary, Robin, and her helper, Sparrow.
Sparrow will take you around and introduce you to the others.
This is Joe; he is an odd bird, always humming something.
This is Jane, always talking about her relative winning a dove award.
This is Wren; she is always feathering her own nest.
This is Jack; be careful, he is a stool pigeon.
This is Joyce; she is always raven about her last review.
This is our boss's office; he is a wise old owl.
We have a definite pecking order here.
Some have flown the coop.
Others are just trying out their wings.
Our motto is "Birds of a feather flock together."
This job is definitely for the birds.

You don't want your trainer to be a mockingbird and mock you.
You don't want them to be a crow and brag about their achievements.
But it is okay if they are a hummingbird and hum while you work out.

How a boss is like an egg:
He can be hard boiled.
He can be scrambled.
He can be over easy.
Around her I have to be an eggspert at everything.
I have to have everything eggsactly right.
All eggs have to be in the same basket.
My boss sometimes has egg on his face from his mistakes.
He is an egghead.
He is always hatching new plans.
We have to walk on eggshells around him.
My boss eggs everyone on.
He likes telling yokes and more yokes.
When things don't go right, he acts like a shell of a man.
I am such a wreck around him, I've been taking Eggslax.

I support the chickens that do the most work; I buy the jumbo eggs.

The Hen House

The place is run by a couple of old hens.
The boss's name is Rooster.
When he crows, people listen.
You can see Rooster fight on Saturday nights.
The booths are called nests, and you can get feather pillow to sit on.
Some young chicks work there.
The hens take them under their wings.
They don't want anyone pecking on them.
They can't be just flapping their wings; they must be working.
Sometimes you hear them cracking with laughter,
and they'll say, "The yoke is on you."
They are not chicken; they stand up for themselves.

The Body

Parts of the body:
You are a sight for sore eyes.
Do you hear what I hear?
You don't want a big mouth.
Woman was created from Adam's rib.
Not very brave; you don't have a backbone.
You don't want to put this in your mouth: foot.
The part of the body God counts: hair.
You are generous; you have a big heart.
The long arm of the law
Hurry up and shake what? Leg.
Ask someone to marry them; get on your knees.
What men have that was named for Adam? Adam's apple.
The cat has got your tongue.
Don't get this in other people's business: nose.
To be smart, use your head.
For solving problems, use your brain.
To end a deal, you shake hands.
French kiss people they meet on the cheek.
Rude people put this part of the hand up: finger.
What you talk: sass. You talking what: lip.
What you shouldn't put on the table: elbows.
When you're with it: You're hip.
It makes you laugh: funny bone.
Part of the body where they drill: teeth.
Part of the body that growls like a lion: stomach

I told a man he looked good for a man of sixty. He told me that he was fifty-five.

Sayings about our bodies:
The idea was on the top of my head.
Hold that thought.
Teachers and mothers have eyes in the back of their head.
I slept like a log. How does a log sleep?
There are too many fingers in the pie. What happened to forks?

It went down the wrong throat. How many throats do you have?
My heart did flip-flops. How does that work?
I got played. Explain.
I won by a nose. Must have a long nose.
My nose is running. Maybe it should enter a race.
I am all ears.
It is on the tip of my tongue.
We are like two peas in a pod.

How mean our body can be.
We give someone a cold shoulder.
We turn our backs on someone.
We shake our heads at someone.
We slap them.
We give them the finger.
We raise our fist to them.
We turn a deaf ear to them.
We roll our eyes at them or look down on them.
We shake the dust off our feet at them.
We run from them.
We boot them out.
We kick them.
We turn our nose up at them.
We give them our elbow.
Give them a taste of our sharp tongue.
Give them a piece of your mind.
Give them the evil eye.
Stare a hole in them.
Give them a dose of their own medicine.

The Head
Don't be headstrong.
Don't be empty headed.
Don't be bullheaded.
Two heads are better than one.
That's where we get the term "double-header."
Don't get a big head.
You're in over your head.
You give me a headache.

Head of the company.
You can go to the head of the class.
You have eyes in the back of your head
You are headstrong.
You have a head cold
You're head over heels in love.
You can give a yes or no answer with
your head by nodding or
shaking your head.
You are headed the wrong way.
Bump heads together.
Use your head.
Isn't your head screwed on right?
You have a lot of head knowledge.
Heads up.

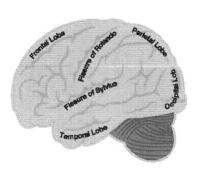

Parts of the Body That Can Be Removed
I got your back.
I want all eyes up here.
Give me your ear.
The cat has got your tongue.
Your nose is in my business.
From my lips to yours.
You got my heart.
I give you my hand in marriage.
I have to catch my breath.
My teeth aren't true but are false.
I can take off my rug wig.
Don't lose your head.
Your mouth fills the room.
You put your foot in your mouth.
My legs just took off on me.
My little toe went to market.

We want people to see us in a certain way and we want to be seen this way, so to help my image my new nickname is Slim.

I hate it when one part of the body gets ahead of the rest of the body. The other day my nose started to run and I couldn't catch it.

I have pants that I haven't worn in months. I tried them on the other day, and they have all shrunk. I may sue the clothing manufacture.

I am beside myself.
I have to find myself.
Look in the mirror.
I am not myself today. Who are you?
I have to find my inner self. Does he live inside your?

My cousin's daughter is really round shouldered and hunches over. To help her she sent her to the program call "Scared Straight." Now her posture is perfect.

I felt so low, I went from singing tenor to singing bass.

Warm versus Cold
I am warmhearted.
I am hot to trot.
I am running a fever.
I got hot hands.
I have hot lips.
She is hot.
I feel like I am on fire.
I have to have potholders with me when I am too hot to handle.
I am coldhearted.
I gave them a cold stare.
I gave them the cold shoulder.
I have a cold.
I am working on a cold case.
Don't get cold feet.
I yell at someone as loudly as I can. I say that I am trying of throw my voice and wonder if they caught it.

A man was running into the grocery store, all out of breath, and his face was red. When asked what the problem was, he said nothing, that his wife just needed him to run to the store.

When you shake your head really fast, you are having a brainstorm. When your head just floats along, that is a brainwave.

Put your leg up. Shows you always wanted to get a leg up on the next guy.

A short person and a tall person went out. That is the short and tall of it.

When my relatives went on trips, they always took my cousin along. It was because he always had a lot of gas.

You put your head ahead of your body and say you're headed out.

Bugs

The roaches are so big in my daughter's apartment, she either has to get rid of them or pay a pet deposit.

It is bad enough I don't get invited to any parties on our street, but twice when I came home at night and turned the garage lights on, I found the water beetles dancing and having a party in the garage.

I am going to do a pilot show on the *Animal Channel* called "What's Bugging You?"

When we say big, we mean big in Texas. The other day I saw two water beetles running off carrying a watermelon.

One night ants were on the floor by our bed. It was our bedtime, too. Sure enough, the ants were going to bed, only it was our bed.

Another time they were lined up two by two in our cupboard. I said to my wife, "Isn't it cute? They are getting a snack before they go to bed."

One time I found bugs in the pantry. Let this be a lesson to all bug people. If I had only left some cookies or crumbs on the table or floor, they would not have had to go to the pantry to look for something to eat.

Know your bugs:
Which one do you take to bed with you? Bedbugs.
Named for a famous British sport: cricket.
Jumps all over the lawn: grasshopper.
A way to get somewhere: fly.
Likes your clothes: moth.
Name of a group of people: wasp.
A good grade: bee.
Like a relative who likes picnics: ant.
Name for a famous motel: roach.
Like matches: firefly.
This bug means the end: termite.
Both the male and female carry this proper name: ladybug.

We say this to get rid of them, but others name a pie for them: shoo fly.

Bug talk: a Jersey boy talking.
Wasps up?
To bee or not to bee? Shakespeare sure knows his bees.
Ant that something?
Benny was always bugging me and putting a flea in my ear.
I got a cricket in my neck from turning around so much.
The teacher said to zip my lips and close my fly.
She sure knows how to tick me off.
She said that way I was going I was going to be a social butterfly,
whatever that means.
She said, "You need to get back to reading about the web that a
spider wove."

Caution: If you have small children or teenagers, are they are acting like pests?
When the pest-control person comes, he will not take away your pests. I know
because I have tried.

Cars

The engine is the heart of the car.

When a car gets excited, they rev up their engine and are roaring to go.

Now sometimes they get too excited and go a little fast, but it is hard for them not to want to show off.

Before they go too far out, they like to shower at a carwash.

If they like another car, it is difficult to keep them apart. They want to go bumper to bumper.

They really dislike it if another car tries to cut in.

When a car cries, it leaks oil.

If they get too excited or like something, they tend to want to honk.

If a car is hurt and in the hospital, you may want to bring them a quart of oil to cheer them up.

People who go from car to car are considered car hopping. This does not please a car.

Sometimes the car is ready to do something but their timing is a little off.

If they get slow and sluggish and don't seem to have a lot of energy, you'll want to check their battery; it is usually low.

At night they like to shed some light on what lies ahead.

When they get old, they get tired and even have some bald spots.

They may even get a little cranky.

Sometimes they are minding their own business and cruising along when other cars come up and start something.

Sometimes a car just needs to be jacked up.

Sometimes they eat too much; they can be a gas guzzler.

At times when they are acting up, you need to see if they have a screw loose when you hear a rattle.

When they get in a fight, you can tell by their dented fender.

If they think you are going too far with them, they sometimes put the brakes on. They don't mind a hands-on relationship with your hands on the wheel.

Careers

A garbage man says he doesn't just kick the can down the road; he picks it up.
"What goes around comes around" is the motto they use for recycling.
He says he doesn't like to get dumped on.
Your treasure later becomes their trash.
He seldom calls in sick because when he has a cold and
can't smell, that is a plus for his job.
Their theme song is "Bin There, Bin Here, Bin Everywhere."

Things to look for in repairing a house:
You don't want a carpenter that screws you.
An electrician that shocks you.
A carpet layer that lies like a rug.
A roofer that short shingles you.
A television repairman that doesn't give you the whole picture.
A painter that brushes you off.
A plumber that is a drip.
A gas man that brings his own natural gas.

Airline pilot:
To have a safe takeoff, it is important to go over the rules of life.
My wife is my copilot, and together we have gone through some rough weather
and had some bumps in our relationship.
We didn't have any turbulence until we had teenagers.
I would tell them to straighten up and fly right.
It is hard when you are so high up not to look down on others.
Sometimes it takes a lot practice to land safely, and I don't always know what
to do, so I just wing it.

My nephew lost his job in a shoe store. They said he was acting like a heel.

My other nephew was a ventriloquist on a cruise ship. They had to let him go.
The audience couldn't figure out which one was the dummy.

My nephew got a job as a crusher at the post office. He gets to jump on the boxes and see if there is anything fragile in them.

My nephew was a storm chaser, but he thought it was too dangerous, so now he is a skirt chaser.

My nephew got a job working for a real estate company. He throws stones at houses to prove they are just a stone's throw away.

An ad for a new haircut place tells us to let them work with your head of hair, and if you're not satisfied, you can get a free cap. Talk about a win-win situation.

Tools
Someone who takes advantage of someone screws.
Used in literature, saying what a man am I: wretched.
Used by dentists to pull teeth: pliers.
Used in magic acts: saw.
According to this song, you do it in the morning and everywhere: hammer.
Hit on the head: nail.
An un-Christian virtue: vice.
What you carry the tools in around your waist: the tool belt.
Dive into a project or what: plunge.
You use it for success: climb a ladder.
Pirates use it to punish people: walk the plank.
Use this to see how you are doing: ruler tape measure.

I find that the more I read, the more I realize how difficult writing is. My friend said I should go to a ghost writer, but the problem is they are hard to find.

My Aunt Edith sings and plays the piano so badly, she got a job where they use her to clear out parties. When she plays and sings, everyone starts to leave.

When you are married to a carpenter:
The first thing he puts on is his tool belt.
He is always worried about getting the shingles.
He always has an axe to grind with someone.
He is always hammering a point home.
He never quits arguing until he hits the nail on the head.
He is always giving out rules and seeing how everyone measures up.

He threatens to make us walk the plank.
He thinks he is levelheaded.
We think he has a screw loose.
He doesn't think he has a vice.
He feels sorry for himself and says, "What a poor wrench am I."
We like it best when he sleeps and we hear him saw.

The baker:
He can rise to any occasion. He is always on a roll. He has lots of dough.

It is not easy to be a wrestler's son in school. They always get in trouble for asking other students if they want to fight and practicing their holds on them.

Hair place:

It is a cut above everywhere else.
They know how to part your waves.
They can get your head straight.
They can wash all your problems away.
They can put a little color in your life.
They can give you some excitement with some highlights.
They know the long and the short of it.
They can chew gum, talk, and go chop-chop all at once.
They want you to feel like you're permanent with them.
They can get to the root of the problem.
They do a bang-up job.
They have some hair-raising days.

Laundry:
Do you feel like you have been hung out to dry?
That you are coming apart?

That you are washed out and have been through the ringer?
That you have some pressing needs?
That you need to clean up your act?
That you don't like the way things smell?
That you have some stains in your life?
That your load is too heavy to bear alone?
You have been hiding a lot of dirty laundry.
Then you need to be taken to the cleaners.
Lucky Lee's Cleaners, where we can put some starch back into your life.

A plumber's lament:
I felt like my life was in a sewer.
I was in the cesspool of life.
The constant dripping of the faucet reminded me of my wife's nagging.
I was blamed by for friends for leaking secrets.
I dreamt I was in a toilet bowl and couldn't get out.
It seemed I knew pipes better than people.
My best friends were Tidy Bowl and my plumber's helper.
I had to get rid of the garbage in my life.
I worked hard to unclog my pipes so I could feel free and breathe again.
Finally after five months, I was able to flush it all down the toilet.

Gambling man:
He was the salt of the earth except for his gambling problem.
He called his horses names like Sugar, Buttermilk, and Pumpkin, names he
should have been calling me.
He always made sure they had their oatmeal every morning.
He said not to worry about things because he brings home the bread.
Some people thought he was crackers.
He had to butter up to people to get information.
When he knew something, he had to be careful not to spill the beans.
He would relish every game.
He was cool as a cucumber.
When his horse lost and he owned money, he would find himself in a jam,
then his legs would shake like jelly.
He knew if he didn't come up with the money, he would be toast.

Why former football players get hired in a company:
They can tackle any problem.
They can catch anything thrown at them.
They know when to run with the ball and when to pass it.
They know there are times when they need to kick the ball down the field.
They work well as a team in a huddle.
They try to avoid penalties.
They have a goal in mind.

It is a good year for little people because I hear they are hiring a smaller work-force this year.

A man said he was not scared of his manager.
He wasn't too afraid of his boss.
He didn't even seem too shook up when the district supervisor came by.
But he was shaking when the terminator came by.

A guy said his brother was a boxer. To show his support for his brother when he had a match, he wore his favorite boxers.

A pastor would preach so long and be so boring, he would put many to sleep. Halfway through his sermon, he would pause and say, "You may now shake your neighbor."

A man worked as a fire eater at a sideshow for many years. He had to quit when he suffered from burnout.

Investors:
One is over his head.
One has a good head for figures.
One has a nose that can smell a good deal.
One has no backbone and is afraid to invest.
One only sees dollar signs in everything.
One has his hands in everything.
One has big ears and hears everything that is going on.
One has a big mouth and tells everyone what is happening.

Railroad engineer talking about his two sons:
One has a one-track mind.

He works to keep his train of thought.
The other is always falling off track.
He is like a train wreck waiting to happen.
The other one is careful not to be on the same track as someone else.
The other one is always in a rush making tracks.
He is always disappearing and is hard to keep track of.
He has to be tracked until he can be caught in a trap.
It looks like one son will be the engineer and the other the caboose.

Chiropractor:

First to say I got your back.
When they are working on two people.
they are working back to back. They say
if you feel out of joint, see us.
Sometimes they laugh with you when
they find your funny bone.
Their favorite food is ribs.
When the chiropractor comes back from
lunch. the receptionist says. "He's back.
They are a touchy-feely type of person.
They believe in a hands-on experience."

Parents tell their children:

A pilot wants his child to have a good takeoff.
A doctor is concerned about the wellness in the child's plan.
A photographer wants to see the total picture.
A cop lays down the law about the right way to go about doing things.
A tailor wants to make sure we don't sew any wild oats.
A broker says he has a lot invested in us and wants to make sure he has a good
return.
A father in construction wants to make sure we don't dig ourselves into a hole.

Weatherman:

I am Larry, the new weatherman. Around here people usually call me
Larry. That is spelled L-A-R-R-Y for those of you who went to public
school and have trouble spelling.
The temperature is 62 and it feels like 62.
There are some highs and lows today, but then aren't there some

highs and low every day?
It might rain tomorrow.
Then again, it might not.
We just have to be patient and wait and see.
I know with these clouds and overcast skies we have been seeing,
some of you have become gloomy and depressed.
Let me tell you, the sun will come out sometimes.
Of course I don't have my crystal ball, so I don't know when the sun will come out.
But be it on the record that Larry said the sun will come out, and
when it does you smile and think of me.

Work in a circus:
Many times we are flying around, looking for something to grab on to.
We often have too much to juggle.
Our boss uses a whip to get us in line.
We have trouble with our balancing.
We are told not to horse around.
We try not to make a monkey of ourselves.
Our boss roars like a lion, and we try to calm him down.

Life as a Clown:
Others often laugh at us and say when they see us, "Here come the clowns."
It is not easy being married to a clown.
Everyone thinks because he has a red nose he has a drinking problem.
You don't know how hard it is to get shoes that are larger than normal sizes.
Company doesn't like to come over anymore; he is always showing his fake
flower, and they are tired of getting wet.
We can't go for a normal drive without him trying to see how many people we
can get in the car.
It is embarrassing to see him ride a tricycle on the street and blow his big horn.
People say to me with disdain, "Oh, you are married to a Clown."
He complains that nobody take him seriously, but everyone just laughs at him.

In writing a story:
A carpenter wants to build on the plot.
A painter wants to make sure you have a clear picture.
A teacher wants it to be a teachable moment and you learn a lesson.
A plumber wants to make sure nobody leaks the plot.

A fisherman usually stretches the truth.
A fireman wants the story to be a hot one.
A newspaper man wants to make sure of the facts.
A banker, in the interest of the reader, wants to keep the ending a surprise.

When a fireman's dog gets too close to the fire, they call him a hot dog.

Detectives keep cold cases in their freezer.
They keep hard evidence in the oven.
They don't have a clue where any food is, so they usually eat out.

I talked to three successful men and asked how they achieved success.
The first pointed to a window with dollar signs on it and said, "That is the window of opportunity."
The second said he keeps a ladder by his house to remind him of the ladder of success he had to climb, starting at the bottom.
The third said he climbs to the top of the house to remind himself he wouldn't be where he was if he didn't stay on top of things.

The Dentist:
I was in a lot of pain, so I went to get help.
He said, "You know the drill."
We will get to the root of the problem.
We will fill in when necessary.
He put a mask on so I couldn't recognize him.
He was getting on my last nerve.
He would talk to me while I could only mumble back.
I left feeling numb.
I also had a big cavity in the pocket.

An office worker's conversation:
Hi Linda, it's me, Marcie. I have been playing that new game, "Lotto Bingo," on the computer most of the morning, and I still can't get the hand of it. Have you tried it yet? I called Sharon and Beth, and they both said they had been trying to do it, too. My supervisor came in and pointed to the paperwork on my desk. He had better not say anything after what I caught him watching on the computer. I don't know where times goes. Here it is, lunchtime already.

A photographer describing his wife: I think maybe she is overexposed.

A psychologist hoping to get the patient more in touch with himself held up a mirror for him and said, "What do you see?" "I see an ugly man holding a mirror." The psychologist said to the patient, "How many times do I have to tell you? No one is following you around at night. It's your shadow."

The psychologist says to the patient, "Why are you here?" The patient says, "Two years ago, I loaned my no-good brother two hundred dollars. My wife said, 'Are you crazy, loaning that no-good ugly brother of yours three hundred dollars?' A year ago, I loaned my brother two hundred dollars. My wife said, 'I cannot believe you are that crazy that you would do that again.' Well, can you guess what I did this year? So I came here."

Some firemen have had to quite their jobs because they can't take the heat.

A man who worked in a box store quit because he felt so boxed in.

Cooking/Food

A letter from my cousin at a booking school describing the staff's reaction to an offer made to them:

It sounds like a raw deal to me.
I think it sounds kind of dicey.
It's an idea that is overdone.
Last time I got a deal like this, I got burned.
Joe was steamed that they didn't ask him first.
Jack came in and, not knowing what was going on, asked, "What's cooking?"
Our Italian waiter said we should just pasta it on the bulletin board
and think about it a while.
The cook was simmering, and I thought he might boil over.
Max, who was peeling onions, said it sounds like a tearjerker.
Mary said if the deal goes through, it will be like icing on the cake.
Joan didn't say anything; she was all clammed up.
So I don't know what we will decide.
Have to go, chop-Chop.

What we know about bread:
We should have it how often? Daily.
Before it's made, it's the same as money: dough.
When you're in trouble, you're toast.
A lazy person: bread loaf.
Some people don't know what side to butter their bread on.
Bread that can be put into the ground: breadsticks.
Bread monkeys like banana bread.
It rises to the occasion.
It can be on a roll.
There is a bun in the oven.

Incident at a meat market:
A man goes up to the butcher.
The butcher says, "I have a beef with you."
The beef is well grounded.

I am tired of you ribbing me
And hamming it up.
You are full of bologna.
You are nothing but a cod.
You are going to a place where you will roast.
I have a lot at steak here.
I have to bring home the bacon every day.
I don't like to flounder around.
I knew there was something fishy about your deal.
Sure enough, the pork went belly up.
And the rest of it was nothing but a big turkey.
You are a chicken.
Come here so I can hit you in your chops
And take a couple of pounds of flesh.

Fruity:
My son is the apple of my eye.
Although often it can be said that he is a crab apple.
He has started to shave and has peach fuzz.
He has a plum job.
He is always looking to the grapevine to see if he can find a better job.
His car has turned out to be a lemon.
His favorite colors are lime green and orange.
Sometimes I think he may be a little fruity.

We are getting ready for our big race:
We had a lot at steak here.
Our opposition was not very nice, as they were giving us the raspberries.
Tom was clowning around and acting like a ham, trying to get us to relax.
Carl was a big chicken and didn't even want to run.
The other team yelled that they were going to cream us.
They yelled, "You will be toast when we are done with you."
Our courage melted like butter.
The other team won the whole enchilada.
We lost so bad that we had egg on our faces.
While the other team went hog wild.

My old friend was working at a food pantry. Before he left, the manager yelled at him to be sure and bring some old bags tomorrow. The next day he showed up with a bunch of old women. "I brought the old hags you asked for."

Food terms that are used all the time:

You are a big ham.

I licked my chops.

You're nuts.

You're full of baloney.

It's no small potatoes.

It only costs peanuts.

Mac brings home the bacon.

Pork bellies refer to stocks.

What am I, chopped liver?

They roasted Virgil at a party.

I have a steak in the outcome.

Don't go cold turkey on me.

You are just a chicken.

Don't fudge your numbers.

It's like taking candy from a baby.

You're toast when I am through with you.

He was smashed flatter than a pancake.

When I was young, I was told not to waste food. Now the food goes to my waist.

Know your vegetables:

They win the race: beets.

A sore on your toe that needs to be taken care of: corn.

When you can't decide on one vegetable, you use: mixed vegetables.

They lost a fight: black-eyed peas.

They are part of the flower family: cauliflower.

If you are red-headed, you are called a: carrot top.

If you are tall and skinny, you are called: bean pole.

Plants first start to grow: Brussels sprouts.

Don't know what they are talking about: You are full of beans.

The vegetable Bush hated: broccoli.

You step on a bug: you squash it.

If you plant an egg, you get an: eggplant.

What vegetable was in the sun too long: baked beans.

Office job:
I got stuck in a traffic jam.
Our group was as slow as molasses.
Jack acted like a crab about the idea.
Tom was in a stew.
The situation was as sticky as cotton candy.
We had to have all the eggs in the basket.
We would be in a pickle if we didn't succeed.
I hoped it would be a piece of cake.

Presentation:
It was a honey of an idea.
We were berry excited about it.
We felt like a steak about to be grilled.
Some had a beef with the idea.
Other ribbed us about it.
Some thought we were milking the idea for too much.
We worked hard to peas everyone so they wouldn't squash our ideas.
We ducked some questions.
Lettuce like syrup, run with the idea.
Our idea needs to be like a hamburger; we need to pat it down, fry it, and watch it sizzle.

Marie Antoinette said when there was no bread for the people, "Let them eat cake." Now the history books have changed it to be healthier, and it says, "Let them eat carrots."

If our appliances could solve problems, here is how they would do it:
Lamp would shed a light on it.
Iron would iron it out.
Stove would light a fire under it.
Pan would put a lid on it.
Teapot would let off steam.
Freezer would be too frozen up to do anything.
Toaster would just pop up with what it thought.
Can opener would ask if we wanted to open this can of worms.
The refrigerator would give an icy glare.
The blender would say, "We just need to learn to blend in."
Coffeepot would say, "We need to perk up."

The mixer would say, "Let's not get mixed up in this."
The garbage disposal would just take it all in.

My wife is Mrs. Dash. I call her Rosemary. She is the spice of my life. She is the salt of the earth. She is so beautiful, she could be on sage. The only time we disagree is about too much pepper. She is seasonally such as good cook. She says to me, "Cumin over here, you big chicken. I got to rub your neck. I have got to start bouillon the chicken." She says, "Herb, I love you, even with your garlic breath." And I said, "I love you, too, when I smell the onion power on you." We have a love that is going to last a life thyme.

Going on a diet:
Sometimes our body is stubborn and fights with us when we diet. I did so well until I went to sleep. I dreamt I was touring a chocolate factory and tasting the heavenly samples. I woke and my mouth started to water thinking about food. My eyes said, "I remember seeing a cheesecake in the refrigerator." My nose said, "I sure love the smell of bacon and eggs." My legs said, "If I need to go the bathroom, they would walk me by the refrigerator."

Doctors

Tom called his doctor and said he was sick and couldn't keep his doctor's appointment.

A bone doctor,
Talking to his child,
"I don't want you to become a bonehead."
You need to bone up on your studies.
Be careful not to pull any boners.
When you make a mistake, don't try to bury your bones.
You need to eat more and put some meat on your bones.
Have a backbone and stand up for yourself.
I will give you some help and throw you a bone now and then.
I want you to get a bonafide degree.

To a patient after going through a checkup:
Have you thought about making a will?
You have the body of a seventy-year-old. Unfortunately I know you are only fifty.
Don't worry if you don't pass the tests the first time; we will give them to you again.
I have got some new pills, and I want you to be the first to try them out.
Now I know the medicine says if you take it, it might make you sick, but then you can always see me again.

I got confused and took my bedtime pill in the morning, so they only thing I could do was to go back to bed so the pill would work.

The doctor had the patient laughing so hard, he left him in stitches.

The nurse had to quit her job because she just didn't have the stomach for it.

People are dying to get out of hospitals. Now they even have an office for those going called "Checking Out."

When I was in the hospital, they would give you a sleeping pill and then wake you up all the time. I told the nurse I wasn't getting any sleep. She said,

"Honey, if you wanted to sleep, you should have gone to a motel."

After being in the hospital a while, when I was ready to leave I had double vision. I saw two of everything. When my wife came to take me home, I wasn't sure which one to go with.

The doctor likes to get to the heart of the matter. Often he has a heart-to-heart talk with the patient.

My uncle was getting up in years. The doctor said, "I need to see you every year." He sends him a new picture every year.

My ear was leaking and I was afraid my brains were leaking out, so I had to put cotton in to stop it.

Sometimes the only time I get blessed is when I sneeze.

A man had to buy two pairs of glasses because he was two faced.

I had a colonoscopy. It took a lot out of me. The doctor said he knows how to get to the bottom of things.

The doctor checked the man over and told him he had way too much stress and he needed to get rid of some of the stress. The man went home and told his wife and three teenagers he was leaving them on doctor's orders.

I like the nurse I had in the hospital; she was always patching things up.

My doctor's name is Dr. Dunn.
I said to him, "Are you Done?"
He said, "No," he hadn't even got started.

Overheard before surgery, a nurse asked another nurse if the doctor had gotten rid of his hiccups.

You recognize your doctor as the former server from the steakhouse who used to carve the meat.

The doctor says there is no mistake that he can't sew up.

My sister went to the doctor in great pain. The doctor said to find out what is wrong, they would have to do a lot of expensive tests. She said, "Will I feel better?" The doctor said, "I don't know, but it will sure help pay for the added west wing."

The eyes are so positive because they have it.

You don't want a nurse that nurses a grudge. You don't want a nurse that needles you.

The doctor asks the nurse if she can find his glasses, then says, "Nevermind. I have done this surgery dozens of times, I could do it blindfolded."

I asked the nurse why it was so cold in the hospital. She said it was because they had a lot of hotheaded people there.

The doctor asked the young man how he got his broken bones. He said his longtime girlfriend dumped him and he was all broken up.

The doctor was all done with the surgery. He asked the nurse if she had seen his scissors because they seemed to be missing.

The nurse used to coach wrestling. He says, "Undress and weigh in."

At the hospital they don't have normal coughs; they have whopping coughs.

The doctor wanted to see me so badly. I said I wanted to be just acquainted with him, and not have a relationship with him.

When people don't have their head covered, they risk a head cold. When they don't have a jacket, they risk getting a chest cold. When their feet are covered right, they get cold feet.

When they wear shorts during cold weather, their knees start to wobble and they start shaking in their boots.
A doctor asking someone to pay up tells him to cough it up.

The X-ray technician says, "I can see right through you."

A patient who has kidney stones says to the doctor, "I wish you would quite saying, 'This too shall pass.'"

Bone doctor:
You don't want a bone doctor saying, "That was your lucky break."

The bone doctor says to his patient, "You know that big break you have been looking forward to? It's here."

The nurses and bone doctor were laughing, and someone said they were breaking up.

A lady and her husband were in the hospital. The husband's leg had just been set in a cast, and they were leaving to go home. The doctor told the wife, "You need to take this prescription to relax and this prescription so you can sleep at night." The man hollered, "What about me? I'm the one with the broken leg." The doctor turned to the wife and said, "You will definitely need these pills."

Eating Out

A Japanese couple came in to dine. The hostess said they could sit wherever they wanted. They ended up sitting on the floor in the corner.

What does a liar, a fisherman, and Burger King all have in common? They all deal in whoppers.

A girl at a cafe trips and falls toward a young man sitting at the next table. A friend says, "She is falling for you."

I went to Five Men and a Burger. When I got there, I counted but could only count four men, so I thought if they lied about that, I wondered what else they lied about.

I went to a place called "Smash Burgers," Now you know that is owned by an angry person. I said I would counsel the boss for a free burger.

A man was arrested for assaulting his wife. Later he was let go when he said he just hit her because she was choking.

When they went to the moon, they thought they might run out of food on the way back, so they were told to pick up some cheese on the moon so they could make sandwiches.

We ate at a fairly nice restaurant. I asked the waiter if they took reservations. He said no, they leave the Indians alone.

A sign in a restaurant said: "You are what you eat." Some businessmen came in and ordered hamburgers. Soon I heard a lot of mooing from their table.

I ate some catfish the other day, but the hairs on it tickled me when I ate it.

We ate in a restaurant, and it was so dark we couldn't see the food. The waiter said they had a new cook and it was best this way.

My wife and I ate in a new place. I looked at the menu and asked the waitress what was good. She said, "Go three blocks down the street."

My wife and I ate out.

The bread was so fresh, my wife had to slap it.

The salad was thrown around; they said it was tossed.

My wife's potato had to be done over; it was twice baked.

My potato lost a battle; it was whipped.

I did not like the number the vegetables did; it was a vegetable melody.

My wife's vegetables were beat up; they were black-eyed peas.

My steak was one of a kind. They said it was rare.

I try to leave a good tip knowing good advice is more valuable than money, but they still wanted money.

Waiters judge the customer:

Some are like sheep; they say the food was baaad.

Some are like goats; everything was okay, butt-butt.

Some are like cows with more than one stomach; they yell for you to give them more food.

Some are like pigs; their mouth is so full they just grunt.

Some are like ducks; they yack and quack on the phone or with each other.

Some are like chickens where they just peck at their food.

Some are like dogs where they bark orders at you and if you don't get it right, they growl at you.

You want them to be cats because cats say everything is perfect.

My aunt has a limp. She is a hostess at a nice restaurant. She tells everyone to walk this way. So they get behind her and limp to their table.

A former military man is working at a Chinese takeout place. He salutes and says, "Sir, I just came from the mess hall, and I have three orders of General Tso's chicken to go. Is permission granted?"

I had to take my wife to the doctor the other day. She got bit by a crab. The sign outside the cafe said "Live Crabs." They put up quite a fight when you try to eat them.

There is a new restaurant called the "Rabbit Hole." There are all types of lettuce to eat, and there is carrot cake, carrot salad, stewed carrots, and carrots fixed many different ways. When you come in, a sign says "Hop over to any table."

Things to look for when you eat out:
1. A pizza man is delivering boxes of pizza and the waiter tells the delivery guy to take them to the kitchen.
2. Overhearing the waiter tell the customer they took care of that roach problem two weeks ago.
3. Hearing someone scream in the kitchen. After the waiter returned to the customer, he asked what the problem was, and the waiter said, "Oh, it was nothing; they thought they saw a mouse."
4. You hear the cooks yelling, "Stop that cat before he runs out the door with the chicken!"
5. The waiter brings you a knife, telling you to be careful because it is so sharp it can cut through wood. By the way, your steak will be ready in twenty minutes.
6. The customer says to the waiter, "This fork is dirty." The waiter says, "I'll be so glad when that dishwasher is fixed."

A big man yells at the waiter, "I didn't order a child's meal! Is that all the bigger it is?"

"How did you find your steak?" The customer replies, "Under the lettuce leaf."

You hear the cook sneezing really loudly in the back. The manager says, "I told him not to come in until he was over that cold."

Growing Old

Part of the problem about growing old is the doctor's fault. Earlier in life, they say, "Don't worry about this or that until you reach a certain age." Suddenly you are there and panic sets in.

It is a time when your body goes out more often than you do.

It is like being in kindergarten all over again. You like your milk and cookies and your afternoon nap, and everyone thinks what you say is kind of silly.

You finally reach the point where you know lots of things about life but find that nobody is interested in what you know.

You learn to listen to your body, and it often says, "Ouch!" You have a dance named for you called the shuffle.

When you think about "hip," it is not how hip you are but hip surgery.

God spends less time with you because He doesn't have that much hair to count.

Some older people lose their memory where they can't remember who they aren't speaking to.

The only appointments on the calendar are doctor, dentist, and eye doctor.

You go on trips more in your dreams than you do in life.

You don't always hear your wife, but then lots of men nod and say yes to their wives.

You find yourself watching television with the sound down. Do you really find that you need to hear it?

When I was told the price for hearing aids would be around six thousand dollars, of course I said, "What? I can't hear you."

You find yourself smiling and nodding at low-speaking people and hope they didn't say anything important.

When your memory goes, be sure and watch it so you don't pay the same bill twice.

Your new game is to find whatever you can't find, and this game can take hours. When you don't do something your wife asks you to do, you say, "I didn't hear you."

When your eyesight isn't so good, dusting is done in half the time, and nobody wants you to wash the pots and pans.

You start seeing white boys as all looking the same.

When you're asked your opinion on some clothes, it is easier to lie because you can't really see it all that well.

You find what was in the top part of your body earlier has often fallen to the middle.

You go to a high school reunion and are surprised at how bald, fat, and generally old your classmates are. You wonder if they haven't been taking care of themselves. It is hard to believe you were in the same class.

You have earned the right to speak your mind. Unfortunately there often isn't as much there that we can remember.

You are always prepared to go on a trip because you have bags under your eyes. You find out if you listened to your parents. If you slouch you will be round shouldered, or if you don't frown you will have wrinkles.

There are times that your favorite room in the house is the bathroom, a room you never want to be too far from.

You are finally free from worrying about public opinion about what people may think of you.

Unfortunately you are about to find out that people don't think about you very much at all.

If you are a fool when you are young, chances are when you are old you will just be an older fool.

I can't complain; this isn't true of most older people.

Older people often can be compared to Jell-O; they get set in their ways.

A older man said he no longer has to go the dentist to get his teeth cleaned; he just sends them in for a cleaning.

If you think older people can't run, you have never seen an older person race to the bathroom in an emergency.

Miscellaneous

A restaurant was quite full. A lady at a table got a call on her cell phone. She had a loud voice to begin with, and as she got excited she got louder, and then she got upset and she was really loud. All of the people at the other tables finally quit eating and talking and were looking at her. Noticing them, she put her phone down and said, "People, this is a private conservation."

A guy said his car and phone were both Smartphones and cars, and you put yours down. You say to him, "There is the car, phone, and you. Two out of three isn't bad."

Death notices:
A man had earlier complained about a frog in his throat. Sure enough, that night he croaked.

Another guy, his friends threw him under the bus.

Another one, his wife left him and he lost his job on the same day. It hit him like a ton of bricks.

Another guy took a leap of faith. Unfortunately it was out of a fourth-story window and there was no net.

Another guy died happy. He was tickled to death.

Another guy was very sentimental. He died all choked up.

A girl said she would die if you meet a certain person; you know what happened.

Even though I brought home the bread, our marriage was in trouble.
You see, I drove a bread truck.
My wife thought I was just a loaf.
I could only say poppycock.
She complained what I brought home was always a day old.
She thought she should be in the upper crust.
She accused me of being interested in a Swedish loaf.

Any way you sliced it, our marriage was in trouble.
Then we found out she had a bun in the oven, and we decided we'd stay together and work it out.
Hopefully our marriage can be like whole bread and we can work it out.

When the mother is five foot and the daughter is five eleven, you may say they never see eye to eye.

A boy said his uncle always got to be Santa because he had a big red nose.

An interview with a famous rodeo star: "How did you happen to get into the rodeo?" "I was roped in. I felt like they had me over a barrel. I was steered that way, and that is no bull."

Around Halloween time, the young kids liked to go to this one politician's house. He was not known to have been the most honest person around. The kids would ask to see his closet. They said their parents said there were lots of skeletons in his closet.

A girl tells her sister not to be a chicken but to come out of her shell.

A guy in the locker room threw his sock at another man. When asked why, he said he wanted to sock it to him.

There was a place that wrapped Christmas gifts. When done they said, "It's all wrapped up." That is where that saying came from.

A lady at the grocery store screamed. I asked what the problem was. She said the high prices scared her.

A man with a big beard was in the locker room. I told him that the beard would get hot and itchy in the summer. He said he wanted to shave and didn't like the beard but his wife did. I told him to go to a costume shop and buy her a beard.

The obituaries are now required to tell the truth. The latest one said, "Mary Fraser died after thirty years of marriage, five of them happy."

A granny had an old-fashioned rocker. She would rock away, but then fall off. The grandchildren would yell, "Granny's off her rocker!"

There is a flu throughout the world, but in only one place is it named. It is called the Hong Kong flu.

I have been trying to buy a "Yard of the Month" sign and put it in our yard to make the neighbors jealous.

The president hates my cats and he doesn't even know them. He says he hates fat cats.

A man was running into the grocery store all out of breath, and his face was red. When asked what was wrong, he said nothing; his wife just needed him to run to the store.

A guy wasn't very smart. He could only handle things that were no-brainers.

The favorite song at the prison is still "Don't Fence Me In."

Two women were locked up in a women's prison. The one said to the other, "Girl, you sure do look good in stripes."

Everyone was bragging about their kids and saying what they could do, like speak Spanish or French. Finally one parent said, "Well, my daughter talks mess."

A teenage boy was arguing with his very pregnant mother while his little brother was listening. The teenager shouted at his mother, saying, "Don't have a cow!" as he slammed the door. The younger brother ran over to his mother and said, "I thought you were having a baby."

A man has his identity stolen. After a month, a man give it back to him, saying, "Your life is too boring."

It is hard up North when it is cold. Everyone wears gloves. A southern boy visiting didn't know what to think. When they went inside, they would say, "The gloves are off."

Four ladies talking"
One says she found moths in the closet.
Another says, "That reminds me, I need to clean my closet; it has been two years."
The third says she has so many boxes in the closet that she can hardly walk in there.

The fourth says that the family has been trying for years to get her brother Frank to come out of the closet.

I am expecting a call from the science department. They are studying great minds.

Bald-headed people are picked on. If a bald person lies, they say it was a bold-faced lie. If he wears a wig or puts on a hat, they wonder what he is covering up.

A guy said he was good at picking winners.
Another guy said he was good at picking a banjo.
A third guy said he was a champion corn picker.
The fourth guy hesitated and thought about it and finally said he
was pretty good at picking his nose.

When a Mormon could have three wives, the middle one was called the mid-wife.

We have to celebrate whatever spot we are in. One team was yelling, "We are number 22!"

This girl went out with this guy who was so full of hot air, she suffered second-degree burns.

My aunt's boy was so lazy, all he did was sit in the chair and eat. She called him Lazy Boy. She couldn't get him to change, but she finally came up with the idea of the La-Z-Boy chair.

At a Christmas party, a man was practicing being Santa Claus, and he was saying, "Ho, ho, ho!" A lady overhearing him slapped him and said, "Don't be calling me a hoe."

I usually don't have a second opinion; it is usually a third or fourth.

Men are wearing bright-colored clothes to bring more color into their lives.

A man said he was too slow to be a first responder, but he was a second responder.

A good way to start the day is to jump up and put your right foot forward. That way you jumpstart your day and get off on the right foot with everyone.

Dancing for the stars is nothing for one couple. They dance on their outdoor porch with the starts every night.

A man died who was a midget at 39. I said, "He sure lived a short life." The guy said, "Don't make fun of midgets; my brother is a midget." I said, "Is he your little brother?"

The first compliment Adam gives to Eve: "I notice there is something different about you." She says she is wearing a new leaf.

My wife works with only half a brain. She is always saying, "I have half a mind to…." I wonder what happened to the other half.

Our neighbor was out in his yard working. I asked if he needed any help. I said, "If you do, I will be glad to send my wife over."

A man said when he went to his wife's family reunion, it was like meeting with a bunch of mixed nuts."

My Aunt Lucy was tied up, and the robber asked her where her valuables were. She said, "Untie me and I will help you look."

Joe was feeling so broke and wanted a surprise, so he wrote himself a check for fifty dollars and mailed it to himself. He took it to the bank and the check bounced.

Someone told me I was acting like a perfect idiot. I said, "Please, no one is perfect."

My uncle was so tight, the only thing he gave away was a cold.

Due to inflation, it is no longer a penny for my thoughts but a dollar. And I don't throw in my two cents' worth but my two dollars.

A girl in her twenties said she sure wished she could read minds. She got her wish and now she can't get a date. Every boy she goes out with she slaps and says, "Don't even think that."

When Tarzan first came to America and landed in New York City and saw all the traffic, he looked out the window and said, "It's a jungle out there."

A guy is walking around with his hand closed. Someone asked, "What's in your hand?" He said someone told him to hold that thought.

What do you call an older Egyptian mother? A mummy.

A guy rushed over to his friend's apartment and said that heard he had gotten a dog. His friend said he didn't get a dog but that he went out with a dog.

I tried to help a girl to leave her life of crime. She had on a t-shirt that said "Property of Some College." I said she should take it off and return it.

Life can be like playing poker.
You have to deal with the deck you are given.
You have to know when to hold them and when to fold them. You have to be able to bluff with a straight face.

A guy spilled butter on a girl.
She said he was just trying to butter her up.

It got so cold up North, they had to put the pigs in blankets.

The weather was going to be cold. One guy got it mixed up on what to do. He brought his plants inside and covered his pets.

When this guy's grandfather was in a poker game, he had a hand of four aces. He said, "Don't that beat all?" That is where this saying comes from.

A guy was wandering around the parking lot picking up things. I asked what he was doing. He said he was gathering up his thoughts; they were pretty scattered earlier.

Say "mouth full." I always wanted to say a mouth full.

A father said he used to sing to his kids to put them to sleep. Later he found he had to quit, as it gave them nightmares.

A guy said he couldn't believe he did something so stupid. His friend said he could, as he had seen him do many dumb things.

A young man went on a date with a new girl. He complained to his friend that she couldn't see. His friend said that he had told him it was a blind date.

A man said his Italian relatives couldn't make it for Thanksgiving. There was some problem with the plane. His grandmother had gotten excited and said something about a bomb using her expression, and the authorities thought there was a bomb on board.

A man said his nephew was in a rock band. He said his band really knew how to move the crowd. When they started playing, people couldn't get out of there fast enough.

My one uncle has so little to rob, he keeps a sign on his window. "I don't have anything. Try next door." The other uncle has so little that after a robbery, they couldn't find anything worth taking. They left him twenty and told him to buy something worthwhile.

My wife says we don't dress up and go out much anymore. One day I surprised her. I said, "You get dressed up, and we will go out and meet new people and have lunch with them. You can pick which funeral you want us to go to."

A man lost over one hundred pounds. His friends said he is not half the man he used to be.

You probably recognize me from *Sports Illustrated* as the famous bowler "Lucky Strike." I used to hang around with Pinhead and Double Lane. Later I would go in the alley, where a man asked me if I could spare a dollar.

A man said he could hardly eat at his family gathering. "Everything," he said, "was wrong, and they kept saying, 'Bite your tongue.' It was so sore."

A single mom was struggling with her three little ones. The pastor preached on, accepting the responsibility of helping others with their burdens. The next Saturday, she left them at the pastor's office, saying she would pick them up at the end of the day.

A man went to a concert. The place was crowded. He sat by a lady and they visited a while. He got up to leave, and she said, "Do you want me to hold your seat?" Putting his hand on his seat, he said, "I don't think we know each other that well."

A friend said he doesn't have to work out. He said he is always jumping to conclusions and running in circles.

It was winter and my uncle was coming up from the valley in Texas, where there is seldom snow or ice. We waited and waited for him for dinner. I asked what took so long. He said he stopped on the bridge and noticed the sign "Watch for ice," and he had been watching for over an hour and hadn't noticed any ice.

A man weighing around three hundred pounds came into the bakery. The baker said, "You are our biggest customer so far."

They said to lose weight, you not only have to work out, but you have to watch what you eat. So I have been taking a mirror with me when I eat out. I don't think I have lost a pound this way.

During the Second World War, the Air Force used two suicide pilots who would go on missions with no chance of coming back. Today if they went, it would be different with the politically correct thinking. A pilot going on a suicide mission would be told to get rid of his cigarette, saying, "That will be the death of you."

It isn't so bad that I watch television with the sound down. The problem is when I try to listen.

Games:
Before you can work for the CIA, you must learn to play "I Spy."
Before you can be a detective, you must know how to play "Clue." If you want to know about living, you must learn to play "Life."
To get into someone's computer, you have to know how to play this game: "Password."
Lots of people want to control everything or play "Monopoly."

I had a moustache when I was younger. It was so blond, nobody knew I had one, so they didn't notice when I shaved it off. Another man said that people thought he had one and it made him look older because he drank a lot of milk.

Colors:
I have a green thumb from working in the garden.
Sometimes I hurt myself and am black and blue.
People accuse me of brown nosing to get closer to my boss.
When I am upset, I turn red.
When I am sick or scared, I turn white.
My hair is turning gray.

I am as squeezable as an orange.
When I am pleased, I am tickled pink.

There was a holy man at the club. He had holes all over his jeans.

In the locker room, a man threw his towel on the floor. He said he was throwing in the towel.

Zelda, the great mind reader, was performing on a cruise ship. During the show, she picked my cousin out of the audience. "Soon I will tell you all your thoughts and what you are thinking. You must try harder; Zelda will soon know all." Finally she said, "This has never happened to me. I just get a blank." I shouted out, "Zelda is great! You got it right!'

A robber approached my uncle and said, "Give me your billfold."
"Why, did you lose yours? I can help you look for it."
"Just give me your wallet."
"You wouldn't want it. It's at least ten years old. I can give you the address of a store where you can get a new one."
"Don't get smart with me, just give me what's inside of it."
"I can't; the credit cards are all in my name and won't do you any good, and you won't know anyone in the pictures."
"Just give me some money."
"Well, you don't need to be so cranky. Here's a five; go buy yourself a cup of coffee."

Every Halloween as kids, we use to go to Old Man Martin's house. He was bent over and used a cane. When he opened the door, he had on the scariest mask we had ever seen. We all screamed and ran away. Only when I was in high school did I find out that Old Man Martin didn't have a mask on.

A man was standing on the sidewalk, shaking his leg. He said his wife told him to hurry up and shake a leg.

A retired military man and his wife retired. She couldn't see too well. She spent all her time nagging him to do this and that. He took to wearing camouflage clothing so she couldn't find him.

The different ways people compliment someone:
A tailor: "You had me in stitches."

A prison guard: "You were a riot."
A bird watcher: "You were a hoot."
A pilot: "You really took off."
A doctor: "You have a really good shot at being a success."
A mortician: "You really brought life back into the program."
An usher: "You had us rolling in the aisles."
A mechanic: "You really knew how to rev up our engines."
A demolition man: "We were all falling down."
A banker: You are really going to bring in the dough."

Roads and highways:
It is either my way or the highway.
Hit the road, meaning get lost.
Crossroads of life.
All reads lead home.
Turn around on the turnpike.
Path to happiness.
Lovers' lane.
Dig up dirt on someone.
In the pit (gravel).
One way.
Life throws a curve.
Bumps in the road.

Making a call to a company about a problem:
Si habla Spanish or English, push button number one or two.
Push number three if you want to pay your bill early.
Push number four if you want to know how much you owe.
Push number five if you want to borrow more money.
If you want to talk to someone, hang on the line.
For the next hour, they play the music "To Dream the Impossible Dream," knowing what little chance you have of talking to anyone.
Finally someone answers. You tell them what you want.
They say they will connect you to the right department, and immediately the connection is lost.
About right now you imagine they are having a good laugh.

Uses of mud:
Stick in the mud.
Here's mud in your eye.
Mud pies.

Mud bath.
Mud slinger.
Don't muddy up the water.

When two employees don't get along:
Batted their heads together.
It finally came to a head.
The one got the other in a headlock.
The head guy caught them.
He said he should knock some sense into their heads.
He said, "You are giving me a headache."
He said to the one, "Don't be so empty-headed."
To the other, he said, "Don't be so headstrong."
"If you two don't get along, you are headed out."

When a carpenter writes a story:
He always likes to build on a good plot.
He likes to have a good foundation.
Some things are set in cement, and he won't change them.
He is very concrete about what he wants.
There is always a measure of suspense.
He likes to knock the walls down between people.
He likes to give more room to his main characters.
He has risen to a high level in his writing.
He has certain points he likes to hammer home.
It is great when he has a clean sweep.
He likes to keep an open window so people can look in.
You won't get board reading his books.
He likes to have a roof over his setting.
He loves it when people get the plot and nail it home.

I am like a bottle of grape jelly and toilet paper. We are all squeezable.

A young man suddenly goes blind. You know what they say, love is blind.

Family get-togethers:
Our family is like Family Feud.
When they get together, it is like a bunch of mixed nuts.
There are the outlaws and the in-laws.
There is the good and the bad, and when they get together it turns ugly.
Our family is like a zoo.

Aunt Mary has a memory like an elephant and doesn't forget anything.
Her kids climb all over the furniture and act like monkeys.
Uncle Ned sticks his neck out and says whatever comes to mind.

A boy said the fight wasn't his fault. He just did what the sign said. The sign said "Reach out and tough somebody."

Some people work for peanuts.
Some people are like this candy: suckers.
This candy is worth a lot: mint.
This candy is very helpful: Lifesaver.
This candy is named for someone very clumsy: Butterfinger.

Manager of a store arguing with a customer: He says you are at least seventy percent off.

Being good as a child when your parent is a baker, you earn brownie points.

Sign at an ice cream shop: "Lick it up and don't be a drip."

Sign at a daycare center: "We take care of your baby from one end to the other."

A grocery worker got fired; they say he got canned.

Trainer talking about his body says he is running a little behind.

A college professor said he was so bright, the students had to wear sunglasses in his classes.

An auditor after looking at the books says things just don't add up.

A hair stylist quit, saying she just didn't feel cut out for the job.

A phone operator said she was discouraged because she had too many hang-ups.

A gas station owner, upset with his employee, says, "Don't be a dipstick."

A music teacher works hard to keep everyone in the right key.

When they say in Congress they haven't read the bill, it shows way too many have gone to public school and are ashamed to admit they can't read.

We say don't trust lawyers, and just what profession are most of the Congress-men and women who are sent to Congress? Lawyers.

A flake when they get older: a frosted flake.

An emergency center got a call. A girl called and said it was a week before the prom and she still didn't have a date.

Asking a fisherman, "What is your net worth?"

A girl goes out with this guy who says he makes lots of money. She did know until later he was part of a counterfeit ring.

When firemen get excited, they are FIRED UP.

Practical Advice:
When you can't see things clearly, clean your glasses or get an eye checkup.

When you have gum on your shoe, you might need to watch where you step.

Your load is too heavy. Open your arms and let some things drop out.

When everything is a mess, it is time to clean house.

Feel as flat as a flat tire: learn what you can do to pump yourself up.

Keep striking out: may need to learn a new game.

Coming unglued: look for what can glue you back together.

When sitting on a gold mine, you may want to get up. That can be rather painful.

Truth has to be told on all signs. Instead of "Men working," a new sign says "Men loafing."

Painter to housewife: "You may want to get a throw rug to put over that spot on the carpet where I spilled paint."

Boss to employee: "You know that retirement you have been dreaming about having some day? Well, the day is here."

Barber says to customer: "Don't worry, it will always grow out."

A lady wrestler telling how she got her husband: She had to put a lot of holds on him and finally pin him down until her agreed to marry her.

A choir member left choir on a sour note.

A man said he was a member of a mob family, but they didn't get any attention because they weren't organized.

A twelve-year-old boy just sat around and played games on his phone. His parents told him he needed to get a hobby. "Get something to collect." He got upset and said he couldn't think of anything for a hobby and went to his room and pouted for an hour. When he came out, he said he had a hobby, and with both Christmas and his birthday coming up, he told his parents they had to promise to get him something for his collection. The parents agreed and asked, "What are you collecting?" He said, "One hundred-dollar bills."

Advice from a laundry worker:
Don't be so stiff like a shirt that has too much starch.
Learn to lighten up and relax.
Don't spend so much time worrying about the spots on your life or clothes that won't come off. If you are too worried about them, wear a sweater or jacket and get on with life.
Soak up all the good things people say to you and the good things that happen during the day.
Rinse off and shake off those irritations that tend to be make you tense and crabby.
You don't want to hang your dirty laundry out so everyone can see your problems.
Wipe those suds or tears out of your eyes.
Remember, everything will come out okay in the wash.
Don't accept the wrong tag people may want to be put on you.
If you do something wrong, come clean and admit what you did.
And above all else, learn to press on in life.

Movies

They are doing remakes of old movies. The one is titled "The Man Who Was Not There." It is renamed "The Man Who Was Not All There."

An actor was scheduled to star in a remake of the movie "The Thin Man," but he gained thirty pounds over the summer, so he didn't get the part.

A friend was in his first play. He had to learn his lines and remember which way to walk off stage. He said if that wasn't enough, his director told him to break a leg. As if he had time to do that, too.

The most dangerous film ever made was "Running with Scissors." Every parent has told their child, "Never run with scissors."

In that one movie that had the man with scissors for hands, his mom used to say he was such a cutup. Imagine his trouble on dates, where the girls would say, "Keep those scissors to yourself." Think how many Band-Aids they used.

I have some cousins that started in movies. One had such big feet, he started in a remake of "Big Foot." The other one played a movie star who had lost so much weight that when a hurricane came through, she blew away. That one is called "Gone with the Wind, Part Two."

My nephew started in his first play in high school called "Clueless." He didn't have to act to fit the role. He later wrote from New York City and told us he finally made it to Broadway. He was on the stage. When the play was over, he swept the floor and put away the props.

I am trying out for a part in "Scream 6." I scream really loudly. It is a silent scream. Did you hear it? The scream is so loud, it can only be heard by dogs. If you heard it, I get to say, "You dog you."

The movie "Little Women" is about midgets.

My nephew, who is so overweight, is trying out for role in the big fan.

Movie titles and what they mean:
"My Darkest Hour": the night the electricity went out.
"Running on Empty": when you ran out of gas.
"My Wife Ran Off with My Best Friend": She left and took the dog with Her.
"I Made It to Base without My Contacts": It is hard to see when your contact falls out.
"The Night I Got Skunked": You really don't want to know what a bad-smelling movie this is.
"Caught in a Web of Deceit and Lying": a political movie about our government.
"I Was Shot Three Times but Still Lived to Tell the Story": I had to have three shots before going overseas.
"Dazed and Confused": finally a movie about teenagers.
"Dumb and Dumber": another political movie explaining the dumb things they do in Congress.
"My Fifty First Dates": Please, do we really need to know your dating life after the first three dates? Boring, boring.
"The Heavy": another story about an overweight guy.
"The Princess and the Frog": She just couldn't get it right and managed to turn him into a prince.
"The Big Break": a doctor's story of how he treated this man's big break.
"Easy Rider": Be careful; this is used by car dealers to show that their cars are easy riders.
"Hair and More Hair": all movies about hair stylists who have no sympathy for those who don't have hair.
"The Good, the Bad, and the Ugly": You don't want to get started on this one. That is about the different teachers a guy had.
"The Night of the Storm": This is a scary story about a man who gets caught by his wife in a big lie.
"Overkill": This is story about how Hollywood uses the same themes over and over again. You definitely will fall asleep in this one.

"The Rubdown": a story about a massager.

"Out of Sight": another story about an invisible man.

"The Longest Night": when you have to sit through another boring movie.

"Planet of the Apes": when a bunch of college football players party.

"Panic": what all college freshmen do when they have a paper due tomorrow that counts as a third of their grade and they haven't started writing it.

"Out of Sight": when you want your teenager to do some work for you.

A man finally got a starring role in a movie but didn't feel he got the recognition he deserved. He started in "Invisible Man," but nobody remembers seeing him.

A man and his wife were at the movies. Before the show started, he decided to go back and get a drink and some popcorn. When he came back, the show had started and it was dark. He sat down and put the popcorn between them so they could share. A little later, he noticed this lady turning around like she was looking for someone. Sure enough, it was his wife.

A guy thought he was a movie star.

He was always causing a scene.

His friends said he was just putting on an act.

The only curtain he over pulled was the shower curtain.

He told his wife she could have a supporting role.

He was always trying out for parts in a movie.

Once he had jelly and honey all over his fingers. He was looking to be a part for "Sticky Fingers, Part II."

He walked around for a week, acting like an ape, hoping to get into a movie about apes.

Finally he got his break when he got a small part in "Monkey Business" with all his monkeying around.

He gets to grunt and climb all over the furniture.

His mother said, "That isn't acting; that's what he does all the time."

When a stranger calls:

Why they don't remake the movie.

A girl baby sitting alone answers the phone.

"Oh, hi, Karl Cameron."

"Say, your voice sure sounds raspy. You may want to get something for it."

"Are you the Karl Cameron that has a big black dog? I think my cousin lives near you. Oh, you have to go now. Well, don't be a stranger."

Why older people aren't hired for movies often:

An older actor is waiting and waiting, and finally they are ready to start shooting. He says, "I have to go to the bathroom now." Later he calls the star Ben, when in the script his name is Pete. He says he was never good at remembering names. Later he is supposed to get excited when someone pulls out a gun. He says, "What gun? I never saw any gun." He finally starts making up his lines. "You know, I can't remember everything."

A young man was going to try out for a part in a movie that was going to be produced in their town. He was leaving when his collie got out and followed him. He didn't have time to take her home, so she had to come with him. After the tryout, they said he wasn't needed but they could use his dog.

Music

The musical group the Icicles:
You get a shiver watching them.
You can feel a cool breeze.
You get cold and want to bring your jacket.
When the leader gives an icy look at the audience, you can see many freeze up.
They really get a chilly reception.
Some give them a cold shoulder.
Their number-one hit is the song "The Popsicles."

As I get older, it is more difficult to remember words and keep up with the music. There is a new group out where you just hum the words. It is called the humdingers.

Singing a song solo: so low, sing very soft.

A famous mountain climber was asked what motivated him to be a mountain climber. He said his mother was a great fan of "The Sound of Music" and would sing the song "Climb Every Mountain."

Music and husbands:
I wanted to be his main squeeze, but he got an accordion instead.
My husband is always fiddling around.
My husband thinks he is a conductor and is always bossing us around.
My husband marches to the beat of his own drum, and we have to figure out what drum that is.
I feel like an old instrument, which he played to get me to do what he wants.
He may know the keyboard but has no idea about the key to my heart.
He plays the strings of the harp but is always stringing me along.
I didn't know when he played the jug; he would get a new one every time and have to drink it dry before he played.
My husband plays the spoons, and you don't know how embarrassing that is when we eat out and often are asked to leave. Mine plays the mouth organ so much, I have decided to become an organ donor.

Remake of a Johnny Cash song:
How high is the water, Mama?
Three feet high and rising.
How high is the water, Mama?
Four feet high and rising.
How high is the water, Mama?
Five feet high and rising.
How high is the water, Mama?
Mama, Mama, how high is the water?
Gulp, gulp.

Song lyrics for "You Are My All in All" (make up your own tune; I gave you the words).
When I lie awake at night, you are there for me.
When I get up in the morning, I am so glad you are by me so I can talk with you.
When we go out to eat, I don't care if I talk to others because I have you with me to talk to.
I would like to spend the whole afternoon with you.
I love it when I go to bed and can stay up and talk to you.
You are my all in all.
Yes, I love my cell phone.

Women in the past didn't know if they could cry or not. The two big songs were "Big Girls Don't Cry" and "It's My Party and I'll Cry if I Want To."

The first song about earthquakes was Elvis singing "I'm All Shook Up."

The song "I Will Follow You Wherever You Go" would now get you in trouble. It would be considered stalking now.

Nowadays you would not be able to hammer in the morning because of noise ordinances.

I am writing a male-bonding song. It is called "I Am in the Dog House." Now you can send me your verses.

I have been going out nights with my tomcat, so when he starts howling I can learn to howl with him. So far we have picked up some money and lots of cans. People can be so rude.

I told my wife, "Get me a mike, and I will be ready to hit the road and be the next big singer." She thinks I have to carry a tune. "Please, you can't do everything." "I have some pretty good moves."

Nowadays it doesn't matter so much what you sound like. You get some good guitars and loud drums, nobody is going hear you anyway.

I go to my first singing practice, singing to the chickens. I was definitely a hit with them.

I tried to be a rap singer, but I just couldn't get the spit right.

A choir director is a very upbeat person. He always likes to end the choir on a high note.

The only song I remember the words to is "Lollipop."

The first song for babies is "Shake, Rattle, and Roll."

A choir directory sang a sharp that turned flat.

A musical group, as it got older, wanted a new name for the group. They all worked out at the gym and wanted a name that identified with who they were and the gym. They are called "The Sitting Dips."

Her husband often sings loudly and off key. She thought she heard him hitting some high notes in the kitchen. She said, "That's the best you've sounded for a long time." He said, "I wasn't singing. I was screaming because I had spilled hot coffee on myself."

Names

A man wanted to name his two children in memory of his pet dogs he had growing up. He wanted them to excel in the names he gave them. He named them Dane and Bernard. You know them as Great Dane and Saint Bernard.

My aunt named her girls after flowers. They were named Rose, Ivy, and Wall-flower.

A man wanted to give his children names where people would want to help them. He named them Goodness and Pete. We sigh for Goodness' and Pete's sake.

A man wanted to give his children names that would be used often. His daughter was given a name that people are asked to say her name. They get quiet when her name is mentioned, and often they bow. Her name is Grace. The boy was given the name used throughout the world. His name is Roger.

A guy told his parents, "I don't really care what name I have; I just want to be named in your will."

A man's nickname for his wife: my little cupcake.
Her nickname for him is her fruitcake.

My wife is called the Queen Bee around home.
You don't want to feel her stinger.

One family lived between Day and Knight.

I went to school with a Hammer and Nails.

Nicknames and last names:
mouse trap
baby doll
cat nap
porky pig
bean pole
bunny hop

Bumper stickers that are hard to find :
My son is a trustee in the county jail.
My son has straight "D's." At least he has something straight.
My nephew is on the honor roll (for those who don't have children of their own).
My cat is a top mouser (for animal lovers).
My dog can beat your dog anytime.

People with these last names are blessed:
Good Knight
Good Job
Done Well
Self Worths
Smart Family
Winners
Eat Plenty's
Good Chance
Good Luck

First words of a lawyer's child: "I'm gonna sue you."
First word of a cashier's child: "Next."
First words of a doctor's child.   He looks at your throat and checks your pulse. "That will be fifty dollars."
First words of a librarian's son: "Be quiet."
First words of a physical trainer's son: "Dad, should we let the fat lady run with us?"
First words of a banker's son: "You can deposit it with me."
First words of a teacher's child: He doesn't have any first words; he just raises his hand and waits to be called on.

Words can have power. Someone says just the word, and he is out of here.

We can choke on our words.
Sometimes we have to eat our words.
Sometimes the word is just on the tip of our tongue.
Some words come back to us when we backtalk.
It can be a blessing when people say they don't know what to say.
Words cannot express how I feel. I am speechless (don't we wish).

Words of action:
go
come
help
stop
run
jump

One guy had it so rough. His nickname was Bull. Everyone put him down. They kept saying, "No Bull, no Bull."

One man named his children after his pets. The girl was Cathy, called Cat for short, and the boy was called Tom.

Norwegian Stories

Times when you should use the Norwegian expression of disgust: "Uff Da":

When the dentist comes with a drill and says, "This won't hurt much."

You have a message on your answering machine that the IRS wants to set up a meeting with you.

You drop your gum in the chicken coop.

You are in a race to get home because you have to use the bathroom and a policeman pulls you over.

You go in for an oil change and the service manager has list of twenty-one things to go over with you.

Your son asks if the school has called yet.

They say your boss is really upset and he wants to see you next.

Your doctor asks if you have made a will.

Your mother-in-law, of whom you are not fond, says she is coming to stay a month.

Instead of winning the "employee of the month," you won the "employee who needs the most improvement."

Story about Hilda and Olaf
Hilda vas a knitting and a knitting.
Olaf said, "Vat you making?"
"I is making you some varm socks so you von't get so cold this vinter."
"I don't ned that. I got my varm underwear and you to keep me varm."
"Ya, vell, this vill be better."
She a yaka and a yaka on the phone for hours.
One time she vas only on for thirty minutes.

I said, "What vas vrong?"

She said, "It vas just a vrong number."

She continued to knit and knit and yack and yack, and my stocking turned out to be long. I now have a long red scarf.

Hilda like to yack and yack.

Her voice was so loud, it sounded like a bullhorn.

She vas giving poor Olaf a headache.

Olaf tried putting cotton in his ears and just nodding and saying yes vhen she talked to him.

But vhen he nodded, it vas not pretty, the chewing out he got.

Hilda said that their nephew Sven had a fight with his vife and she vansn't speaking to him.

Olaf said, "Ay, that Sven alvays vas a lucky fellow."

Olaf and Hilda lived in a poor neighbor. They veer going somewhere vhen my aunt said she had to run into the house to get something. A man stepped out of the bushes and pulled a gun on her, asking for her money. My uncle yelled out, "Vhat's holding you up?"

Norway's Star

Hilda says to Olaf, "Ve need a big tree this year."

Olaf says, "But Hilda, the last time I had to trim the tree so much, it just had a three branches left."

Hilda says, "Ay, but our families vill be here. Ve need a big tree."

"But I had to tie the last one to the railing to get it to stand."

"Olaf, Olaf, I vant a big tree. You vill get me one."

So I took Lars with me and the sled to carry the tree from the Mountain.

Lars is my big and strong nephew.

Ve found a big tree and Lars, he start a chopping and chopping, I say,

"Hurry up!" as I vas jumping up and down to keep varm.

Finally ve get it down and tie it to the sled as Lars is ahead of the sled to pull it.

Suddenly I sneeze and jump and sled starts out on its own.

Lars feel on the sled and the sled raced down the hill vith a mind of its own.

He vas a riding it like a bronco horse and yelling his head off.

It vas hours later vhen I made it down.

Lars had made it down in record time.

From vhat Lars learned this year, he vas able to be the captain of the toboggan team in the Olympics for Noway.

I couldn't be prouder.

A Norwegian egghead tells something funny; he alvays says to the person, "The yoke is on you."

A Norwegian billfold: You put a dollar in, close it, and open it, and the dollar is on the other side. The Norwegian man than asks if anyone would give him a twenty, he could put it in and see if he can get it to disappear. He is still vorking on the part of getting it to return.

How do you spell "heaven" in Norway? Capital N-O-R-W-A-Y.

Olaf has sucha smelly feet. Vhen he had to take his shoes off at the airport, three people fainted.

Police

A man said when he got married, his wife was a police captain. Instead of saying their wedding vows, she read him his rights, stressing the part about "you have the right to remain silent."

She was always bullying him with her club.

She said since she wore the badge in the family, that made her the boss.

When she went undercover and took off her makeup, it was so scary. If she was on the street, she could be arrested for indecent exposure.

My nephew was trying out to be a policeman. His Uncle Bubba, who had been one for twenty-years, said he would show him the ropes. In Texas every third man is called Bubba. He took him to a rundown part of the city. He said, "There is lots of crime, drugs, and gangs in this part of the city. You want to stay away from here. If you get a call, take your time answering. You want to be sure to give the bad guys plenty of time to get away." He put on his siren and showed his nephew how to get around traffic. In the morning, he showed him where the real police work took place. With the police car in a quiet place, hiding behind a tree, he stopped a student who was late for class, another man on his way to work, and a man trying to catch a flight at the airport. "I hope he was able to get a later flight." In a couple of hours, all the work was done. He said it was lunch between eleven and one. "Most of our work is done for the day, so we can meet with other officers and have lunch. Police officers don't eat alone." Later they went to the donut shop, where he was only able to eat three donuts. Bubba said, "Son, you aren't ever going to make it as a policeman." Later my nephew was out driving and saw a sign that said "Road construction ahead" and "Slow men working." Well, being my nephew was kind of slow, he got a job with the highway department, where he designs plans where they can block off most roads, making it almost impossible for most people to get to work.

Dating a policeman:

When I am not ready, he always says, "What's the holdup??"

Instead of just talking to me, he interrogates me.

When I confess to anything, he always wants to record it.

He is always looking for clues to what I have been doing.

I don't know how many pairs of handcuffs I need for my birthday.

The word "Wanted" is on top of my picture.

When I caught him in a compromising situation, he said he was working undercover.

When I questioned him more about it, he said he had the right to remain silent.

Being raised by a policeman wasn't easy.

Instead of reading me bedtime stories, he would read me my rights. He would get so upset if I beat him in the game Clue.

When we played Monopoly, he would get excited when I had to go to jail.

He was always being the good/bad cop. I never knew which one he would be on any given day.

When I did anything, he would say, "Now just the facts. I want nothing but the facts."

When I went out on a date, he would have me tailed.

I would hate it that he would look up to see if my date had a record. It was even worse when he would frisk my date when we came home. I don't know how many times I would have to listen to the song "Jailhouse Rock."

It was a crime the way I was raised.

Two robbers were in jail. One asked the other how he knew which house to break into. He said he looked for the signs that said "Open House."

Popcorn Role in History

It was the time just before the first Thanksgiving. The Pilgrims and the Indians were going to have their first Thanksgiving dinner together. The Indian children worried about the Pilgrim children. They thought they were going to get so tired of leftover turkey, turkey stew, turkey hash, and turkey just about every way you could think of. So the Indian children gave the Pilgrim children popcorn so on the cold winter nights, when they were tired of turkey, they could make popcorn around the fire.

It was a terrible time for the troops under George Washington. They hadn't been paid, they had few weapons, and some didn't even have shoes. It was just before Valley Forge, and the troops were deserting in droves. Washington didn't know what to do to keep them. One soldier whispered something in his ear. Before you knew it, they started to make popcorn around the fire and nobody left anymore.

It was a terrible feud between the Hatfields and the McCoys. It had gone on for years. One day the McCoy girls were making popcorn, and one girl said, "Those mean Hatfield boys are coming, and they are bringing rocks to throw at our house." Being the wise girl, she was the older McCoy, so she said, "Just open the window and set the popcorn on the sill." She yelled out, "Boys, if you put the rocks down, you can all come in for some popcorn." Thus ended the feud.

The Northern soldiers were burning everything in sight. No one was safe. At the one home, the Stone sisters didn't know how to protect themselves or their house. Finally one said, "Let's make some popcorn and invite them Northern boys in for a snack, and we can sing around the fire." Their house was the only one left standing in the whole area.

It was a rough time in the trenches during World War I. There were rats, water, rain, and nothing to look forward to. One soldier's mom sent him some popcorn, and they started a fire and started to pop the corn. Unable to handle the smell, a white flag went up from the other side. They wanted to know what the incredible smell was. So for one night, the Germans and Americans shared some popcorn, and all was right with the world.

They needed to recruit this young athlete for their baseball team. He had countless offers, and they needed him badly. He came from a rich family and money didn't mean much. How could their offer beat the others', who so badly wanted him? They found out that he loved popcorn to snack on. They finally came up with an idea they told him after every game, they make fresh popcorn for the team to snack on. You guessed it, he signed with them.

They were at an impasse, the two sides. The meeting dragged on and on. The two sides could not agree on the main points. Finally a clever secretary went into the break room, made some popcorn, and left the door open so the smell would go into the meeting room. Sure enough, they got things settled so they could all have a popcorn snack.

In the spaceship. they had a monkey along with them to test things. Unfortunately the monkey was getting tired of bananas, and they didn't know what to do; it was climbing all over everything. They called the space station, and one wise man said, "Make popcorn; it will keep the monkey occupied and he will like it." Another space mission saved by popcorn.

The high school was having major problems. Their dropout rate was one of the worst in the city and state. The newspaper wrote horrible articles about them. They knew soon they would have no job if things didn't change. Finally a teacher brought up an idea that was new and hadn't been used. Popcorn was made and delivered to every classroom so the students could munch on popcorn while they did their schoolwork. Need I say there was a dramatic turnaround in their dropout rate.

Relationships

How different women found their husbands to be:
One was outside praying and a skydiver dropped out of the sky.
Another one was in the hospital, and every time the doctor came in to see her, her fever went way up.
Her little brother was playing with matches and started a fire. When the fireman came to put it out, there was a spark between the two of them.
A dance instructor said he just waltzed right in.
A photographer was always trying to get her into focus.
After trying on twenty pairs of shoes, the shoe salesman said, "If this one fits, it's a match."
She dated a sanitation worker who said he didn't like to talk trash.

Judge: "How do you plea?"
"Mercy, Judge, mercy."
I usually get down on my hands and knees.
"Think of my poor wife and children." The lawyer whispers to him, "You are single." "Well, then, think of my sister's kids."
Insanity: Nobody in their right mind would rob a bank at a busy shopping center at noon when it is full of people.

I was having dreams about my latest girlfriend.
Unfortunately they were nightmares.

This man had trophies of animals all over his den. In the middle of them was a large picture of his wife. He said, "She is my trophy wife."

A lady was dating an IRS man, but she gave it up. She said it was too taxing.

A girl met her husband when she would ride the subway in Chicago. He would give her her tokens and say they were a token of his love for her.

The UPS man liked his girlfriend because he liked the package she came in. He hoped soon to tie the knot with her and in a few months have everything wrapped up. He said, "Stay with me. I deliver the goods."

True love between young people: A boy says to his girlfriend as he lifts up his shirt, "My chest is a blank slate, of which you can be the first to write on it."

You can tell we are in hard times when everyone is writing on themselves. Be careful when you are in an accident; the police will want to see your current girlfriends and your name. Nowadays they read the messages on you more than look at your wallet.

My wife is a needle pointer.
She is always needling me.
I say, "What is the point?"
I try to pin her down.
She gets so upset when I say, "Sew, sew."
She is trying to hook me to her side.

Love story about two firemen:
He said, "You are the spark that lights my fire."
"I know we shouldn't, but we both enjoyed playing with matches."
"Think of all the good times we had when we would follow the smoke, and where there is smoke there is fire."
"You would sometimes be so hot, I would back away so I wouldn't get burned."
"Many times I had to hose off."
"We had so much fun roasting marshmallows by the fire of burning buildings."
"I really thought we could climb the ladder together."
"Now you say that our relationship is just ashes, but remember, there is beauty in the ashes."
"You want me to think of you as my old flame."
"But I still have a burning desire to get back with you."

A tree trimmer says to his girlfriend, "I would go out on a limb for you."

A librarian offering advice on relationships says you want to have a good cover in case things go wrong. You don't want to be overbooked. You want to offer some romance and some suspense. You hope she wants to turn the pages in your relationship. At times you have to leave a bookmark in the spot where your relationship has stopped. You want to work on having a good ending to the book.

A mechanic says the key to a good relationship is to keep the heat tuned up.

When things don't turn out for a sportscaster, he always has to go over it play by play to see what went wrong.

You may want to date someone who has been an Eagle Scout. They have a hard time lying because they always say, "On Scout's Honor."

I always wanted a husband who loved to travel and would take me places I had never been. I got my wish. I married a truck driver.

He said he worked with oil. I thought he meant oil wells, not Jiffy Lube.

A butcher says, "Nothing but the prime beef is good enough for my girl."

Describing husbands:
Always spinning tales and blowing his top like a top.
Like a weasel, he is always popping up.
He is like a puppet; he does whatever the person wants him to who pulls his strings.
He is like a crybaby, always calling, "Mama."
He is like a train. He has a lot of steam but is hard to keep on track.

A man says being married to his wife is like living in a chicken yard.
She is always crowing about her achievements.
She always has a bunch of old hens over and they are always clacking.
She is forever picking on me.
She says that I am cheap-cheap.
She says I don't bring home enough money and I need to get out there and lay another egg.
She says I need to save for our nest egg.
When her family is over, I have to be careful not to ruffle any feathers.
She teases me and makes fun of me and says the jolk is on me.
Things are not always what they are cracked up to be.
I feel like I am becoming a shell of a man.

Terms people in different jobs use to describe their relationships:
Mechanic: She is well oiled and ready to run.
Fireman: She is the match that lights my fire.
Policeman: I am ready to book her.

Banker: I have a high interest in her.

Teacher: She knows her ABC's and is teachable.

Forest Ranger: She is ready to come out of the woods.

Lawyer: Where there is a will, there is a way.

Farmer: She has good seeds, and I see a lot of growth.

Politician: I have found my soulmate. She can look me in the eye and tell a whopper of a lie.

When a mailman broke up with his girlfriend, she stamped him: "Return to Sender."

A woman was arguing with her husband, a carpet salesman, and she said to him, "Do you think I am going to take it and lie here like a rug?"

A single man was asked by his friend if he would take his wife's friend out on a date when she came to the city. He was not too interested in doing it, so his friend said she was in a beauty contest. He finally agreed and took her out. Now she had a big nose and was very plain looking. It was difficult to imagine her in a beauty contest. Finally over dinner, he asked her if she was ever in a beauty contest. She said yes, a couple of years ago she was the judge in a beauty contest.

A man worked in the parcel post in the post office, and everyone got a number when they came in to get their packages. His wife, who was very upset, told her best friend, "I am just a number to him."

Cell phone date:
The couple is seated at a table, and almost immediately her cell phone begins to ring. She talks in low tone for a while and then hangs up, and then his phone rings. Finally they order and she goes to the bathroom, taking two more calls. She comes back to the table and finds him talking on the phone. After eating a little and finding very little to say to each other, they leave. He asks her if he can call her at home. She says sure. He calls her up and they talk more than an hour on the phone.

My sister's husband said he may as well have the job of being a mover, because he is continually moving furniture for her.

Being married to a fisherman isn't easy. She would hint things to him, but he wouldn't often take the bait. She would try to trap him in things, but he was slippery. It was hard to reel him in so he would listen to her. She told him to stay out of the tank; it would be a sinker for him.

It is hard to date an English teacher. She corrects all my grammar mistakes on the love notes I send her. If I don't say something right. she says. "Now shall we say that again the right way?"

A client has a crush on a psychologist. She says she is crazy about him.

A counselor says to a client, "I hope you are not going to bother me with any more problems."

My wife is like what we raise:
I raise bees; my wife is a honey.
I have a fruit orchard; my wife is a peach.
I raise sugarcane; I call my wife sugar.
I raise corn; my wife is corny.
I have a dairy farm; my wife is bossy.
I raised horses; my wife is a night mare.

His children are like a deck of cards.
My daughter acts like the queen; we are all supposed to bow down to her.
My son Jack is a Jack of all trades; he can fix most anything.
Tom is my ace; he is at the top of his class and brings home rewards. Jerry is our joker.
The last child is a wild card.

I had to take a cool bath at night because I had been in hot water all day.

The linesman said about his relationship, "Sometimes the lines are down now, but I'm hoping they'll be restored shortly."

When I turn sideways, my profile is just like my dad's; my body structure is short and stout, like my grandfather; my big noise, which I don't like, is just like my mother's; and my kids give me my gray hair.

Before there were gangs, there were mothers.
If the mothers had control over their children, there would be fewer problems.
When the boy asks his mother where the red rag is, she says, "That old rag? It had a stain like blood on it. You must have cut yourself. I threw it away."
I talked to the other mothers, and we all thought you should wear green or brown. You don't want colors that clash with other colors.

Sports

Reasons people in sports can't do something:
A golfer said he was too upset; he was teed off.
Another golfer said he just didn't feel up to par.
A bowler said he was bowled over with too much to do.
A lacrosse played was just horsing around.
A baseball player asked three girls out and they all said no, so he was out.
A football player said he didn't feel like tackling any problems.
A tennis player said he was too set in his ways.
A basketball player said he was busy bouncing some ideas around.
A runner didn't want to come because he was afraid he might run into the wrong person.
A swimmer said he would come but he felt like he was under water.

I was never very good at baseball. The only thing I could ever catch was a cold.

The Winter Olympics:
It looks like it is all downhill.
The skaters are skating on thin ice. Go figure, what is up with that? The Canadians seem to be sweeping up with their brooms.
I am not sure what to believe or wonder if they are just giving us a snow job.

This is the year of the runner.
Many are running for office.
People are getting ideas and running with them.
Some run down the stairs. They are run down.
Some run business.
Some are running in circles.
Some are running out of time.
Some run into someone and others away from someone.
Some are running out of luck.
Some are running with the ball.

My son, the swimmer:
He is always in the swim of things.

He wants to dive off the deep end and take risks.
He does things backward like his backward stroke.
Other times he just floats along.
He always gets a kick out of things.
He takes a lot of strokes just like the way he plays golf.
He likes to make waves.
Basically I think he is all wet.

Baseball player's love story:
I thought this girl would be a good catch.
She always thought I was out in left field and not in the same league as she was.
In order to get to first base with her, I knew I would have to go through her dad.
He said, "If you want to be on our team, give me your best pitch."
I threw him a fastball.
He threw me back a curveball.
This went on for some time until I finally got to be a hit with him.
Now he said, "If you want to get to second base, you have to learn to be patient and wait to walk. It won't do for you to try and steal bases."
When we would go out, we had to make short stops to let him know what we were doing.
If I did something wrong, my girlfriend would say, "That is strike one, and you never want me to get to strike three."
This went on for two years.
Finally I got all the bases covered and felt like I hit a home run when I asked her to marry me.

Playing ball is a lot like working at a job.
If the ball is in your court, you need to learn to run with it or when you need to pass the ball.
Our boss says we have to get on the ball.
Sometimes he plays hard ball with us.
At times we have to learn to dodge the ball.
Be careful not to drop the ball.
Sometimes the others play keep-away with the ball and you have to learn to jump in.
Some just sit on the ball and do nothing.
When I pay my bills, it reminds me of a ball when both my ball and my checks bounce.

After too many strokes, a golfer gets teed off.

A wrestler's aim is to pin down another wrestler, but then it is like all of us at times; we always try to pin someone down.

Stepping:
At first when we start out, we take baby steps.
Then when more sure of ourselves, we take larger steps, learning to step out when necessary.
We learn as we go on, sometimes stepping into messes.
At times we have to step over others.
Other times we may step on someone's fingers and toes.
We step high as we reach for the stars.
It helps having our stepmom behind us.
To reach higher, we may use the stepladder.
Finally we are one step away from being president of the company.

Racket ball is so noisy.

When you play games on your horse, you have to be careful not to just horse around and not to get on your high horse toward others.

In golf you just have to finish the course to see how things will turn out.

Jack was a sore loser; he hurt all over.

Hunter says to his friend, "Are you game? I am going to bring in all the big guns."

When my husband and I are arguing, he is always calling for timeouts.

Guys are talking about past Olympics. One told about how someone broke seven records in swimming. Another guy said he heard about someone breaking five records in racing. The other guy said, "I remember when my nephew broke ten records and boy, was my brother upset with him."

Teachers

Teacher to student: "When I said we need to tie things together, I didn't mean for you to tie Lisa's pigtails together."

Teacher to student: "How come you quit writing halfway through your essay?" Student: "I am a man of few words."

The teacher told everyone to line up. One little boy raised his hand. The teacher said, "Yes, Sammy?" "You know, my father was in a lineup once, too."

Teacher: "How did you get to be so good?" "Chalk it up to experience."

Teacher to student: "Why are you standing on your head?" "I think better on my head than on my feet."

Teacher to student: "How many times have I told you not to walk around and bother other students?" "Miss, you know I don't do well in math. I can't add that many."

A boy to his younger brother: "Do you have to repeat everything I do? Just because I had to repeat fourth grade doesn't mean you have to do it, too."

A teacher to a student about the subject of his paper: "I just don't think it is an appropriate topic to write about: 'The people I want to send on a one-way ticket to the moon.'"

Jack: "Why are you in Mary's seat and not your own?" "I thought if I took her seat, it would help me be smarter."

I know when I asked you what you do best, I was hoping for something a little more positive than "annoy others."

Why you might think twice about taking your sixth-graders on a field trip to the city park:
Joe found a snake and chased others with it.
Lynn picked a plant that was poison ivy.
Two students got bit by ants.

Two others got too close to the creek and fell in.

Cherry got lost in the woods and it took us an hour to find her.

Bill and Jerry thought a skunk was so cute and got too close, and you know the rest.

When we got back to our starting point to eat, two raccoons had already started eating our food.

Larry, if you are going to copy someone else's work, you need to learn how to do a neater job of it.

Boy to principal: "So I slept in class? My fifth-period teacher does all the time."

Travel

How to get around the world with few words:

In Norwegian say, "Jeg snakker ikke norsk."
Norse: "I can't speak Norwegian. They will speak English."

It doesn't hurt to say you know Olaf and Hilda, too, in Norway. Everyone knows an Olaf and a Hilda.

In Germany say, "Ich verstehe nicht" ("I don't understand"), and then say, "Ich Spreche kein English."

In France say, "Bonjour" and "Oui Oui," and if you want to, "Ooh, la, la." If you want to eat, say, "French fries" and "French toast."

In the South say, "Well, I do declare using a slow accent."

In Canada put an "eh?" at the end of each sentence.

In Mexico, if a guy is going to rob you, you quickly say, "Amigo!" run over, and give him a big hug. He will be confused; he will no longer be thinking of robbing you.

Some people talk out of both sides of their mouth.

Talking with a forked tongue can be difficult.

Young people talking about their summer trips.

We always had to go during offseason, when all the amusements parks were closed.

My folks sent me to camp in June and camp didn't start until July.

My father said he wouldn't go without taking the dog, and my mother said she wouldn't go with the dog. In the morning, my father and the dog were gone.

When asked what he did last summer, he handed in a blank sheet of paper. He said he didn't do anything.

This guy loved it that his uncle sent him postcards from all over the world. Of course it helped that his uncle was wanted by the police and had to keep on the move.

We used to go with my grandfather on car trips. He would entertain us, telling about all the close calls he had on previous trips and watching everything but the road. To go with him, you had to be prayed up.

My parents left Chicago at night, on their way west to the Black Hills in South Dakota. It was night and they were arguing all the way, which turned out to be the wrong way. They do have a nice zoo in Toledo.

We didn't take trips, but then our mother was a trip.

Our trips were sort of like a rocking chair. You can sit on the chair and dream and rock as much as you like, but you aren't going anywhere.

My parents fought over where they were going. Dad wanted a hunting trip to Canada, and Mom wanted to go to the beach in the Bahamas. They finally decided to go their separate ways. They were hardly speaking. They went to a marriage seminar at church, and both convicted of how selfish they were being. Not wanting to admit they were wrong but wanting to surprise the other one, Dad went to the Bahamas and Mom went to Canada. Surprise, surprise.

Our family went camping. Because Dad drove, he was very tired, so he went to sleep early. Not wanting to wake him, Mom left the tent flap open and went for a walk. Upon returning, she looked in and a bear was sleeping alongside her husband. Knowing what a grouch he would be if she woke him, she decided to go sleep with the kids.

Werewolves, Vampires, and Zombies

The lady who was married to the werewolf: Did she love the man more or the wolf? If he saw a pretty girl and howled at her, was it okay if he said it was just the wolf in him?

Once in a while, I start howling. I can't stop it. I think maybe I got bit by a werewolf. I think one of my neighbors is a werewolf, but I don't know which one. Meanwhile I have the strangest feeling that I should take a bite out of crime.

What life is like being married to a werewolf from an ex:
We had to buy a new couch every two years, the way his claws tore up the couch.
At night I would say, "Get your paws away from me. I don't want any more scratches."
I thought I would be first in life, but it was always the pack that came first.
I asked him to bring home a chicken for dinner, and he brings a live one home in his mouth.
When I would go to bed at night, I would get phone calls from the neighbors, who complained that he was out howling at the full moon.
Think of our family pictures. There was me with the three kids, standing next to a large wolf. Now that was something hard to explain.

Vampire:
Blood thirsty, need a blood transfusion.
Blood-curdling yell.
They say, "Get your bloody hands off me."
"Who made this bloody mess?"
Bad blood between brothers: One is a positive and one a negative.
Take blood baths.
Drink bloody Marys.
Drive blood mobiles.
See a doctor for bloodwork.
Go to blood banks.
They are blood donors.

New blood when a new one comes along.
Like to keep a pure bloodline.

Zombie:
They are dead to the world.
They look like death warmed over.
They are dead on their feet.
They are deadbeats.

They like their pain deadened.
They have dead-end jobs.
Their favorite music group is the "Grateful Dead."
They say to their mate, "You will be the death of me yet."
They read the death notices.
Often you will find them working at funeral homes.
Remember, they can be deadly.

Signs that someone may have werewolf tendencies:
They like to howl.
They have an excess of body hair.
Their favorite place to visit is the wolf's pen at the zoo.
They get very excited and wound up when there is a full moon.
There favorite movies are "The Howling" and other werewolf movies.
They like to run in packs.
They are very familiar with the woods and never seem to get lost.
If you see any of these signs, call immediately your animal control person.

You will find many of all of the above working in Hollywood or traveling in Europe.

Working Out

Two guys were tossing a weight back and forth. I asked what they were doing. They said they were throwing their weight around.

They said the free-weights were in the back of the gym. I tried to take some out and was stopped at the door. So much for free.

I don't work out by the mirrors anymore. It hurts to see someone work out that hard.

I was going to sue the gym. They said if I worked hard I would have muscles. They didn't say the muscles would all be in my stomach. Now when I want to show off my muscles and wear a muscle shirt. it is not a pretty sight.

The world says don't sweat it, while at the club they say sweat it. At my age, when I sweat too much, it is time to slow down.

Stand behind someone and tell them you have their back. It is better than to front them.

When someone takes a weight and swings it from side to side, it shows they are attention deficit.

Some people say the way they are shaped, they have more behind them than ahead of them.

A guy was hanging from a rod while working out. I said, "What are you doing, just hanging around?" I said, "What is your hang-up, anyway?"

A guy who was considered a pest said he lost a lot of weight. People kept telling him to take a hike and get lost, so he did both.

The trainer was teaching someone to squat the message, which was "I don't give a squat."

Some trainers have others bow down to them. That is so wrong; they have a big enough head as it is.

Others have them curtsy, which is unnecessary when there is no royalty in Texas.

Can't say around the gym: "You carry more weight than I do" or "Don't throw your weight around."

Our club has been promoting vio-lence for women with boxing classes. I told them the women would probably be hitting their boyfriends and husbands. I recom-mended a non-violence class where it wouldn't go past tickling. Then I read in the paper there is a problem with that, when I heard about a man who was tickled to death.

There was a fight in the locker room. One guy said he was trying to whip the other guy into shape.

In the locker room, a man threw his towel on the floor. He said he was throw-ing in the towel.

When someone runs down the stairs, we say they are run down.

When someone jumps up and down and shouts, we know they are finished with the workout.

When someone stretches as far as he can and says, "I am the greatest," that is called stretching the truth.

When someone reaches as far as they can up, we know they are reaching for the stars and expecting a good year this year.

A trainer tells a girl to run as fast as she can, pretending she has ten minutes to use the bathroom before the bus comes.

When someone squeezes a big ball against the wall, you know he is going to put the squeeze on someone next year.

When someone lies down in a prostate position or bows down, you know they are practicing asking their boss for a raise.

When someone lies on one side and then the other, you know they can't decide what side to be on.

If a man carries a big weight and then bows down, you know he is getting ready to get married.

Working out and shrugging your shoulders is called "doing the shrug." You shrug off weight and problems at the same time.

If you lie on a ball and it bounces back, you know that person is getting ready to bounce back this year.

Most don't need practice on how to lay down on the job. But if they do and someone comes by, they wave their leg on them. That is called doing the backward wave.

When someone is bent over and touching their toes, that is being in the hangover position.

The weights in the back of the gym, a guy named for his not-too-bright brother. They are called the dumbbells.

There is a weight named for a dog called the leg lift.

The abdominal crunch is used for pregnant women to help get the baby out.

The bug workouts can be helpful.

The roach: You look around and then run as fast as you can.
The grasshopper: You just hop around.
The cricket: You go down and then jump up.
The butterfly: You just wave your arms and run around.
The spider: You put your arms and legs spread out as far as you can.
The bee: You buzz around and then you get to sting someone.
Some do the leapfrog, where they jump and down from a stool.

When someone carries a lot of weight, has a lot of pull, and knows the ropes, they are ready to face the world.

I told them at the gym I won't help them if they bench press over two hundred pounds; I feel that is showing off.

It is hard when weight leaves all parts of your body and meets in your middle.

A man seemed to have gotten shorter. Someone said he was selling himself short.

If you going to win on the stationary bikes, you need to get a bike in the front roll. Then you can yell, "I am the winner!" and demand a prize.

Remember when working out not to look too happy, but make it seem like you're in pain.

I have helped so many to work out. They aren't doing anything, then I talk to them and they suddenly say they have to run and can't get away fast enough.

I hate it when I am comfortable and doing well and some do-gooder comes along and tells me I am using the machine wrong and wants to show me the right way to use it.

Someone said they lost twenty pounds, and another person said they found it. Remember, the weight that leaves someone goes around until it can find someone else to attach itself to.

Two guys lying side by side and are both kicking, one is called the other's side-kick.

Using a long pole and trying to keep a balance if they slip, people think they are off balance.

If someone lifts a ball high, that's called a highball.

If someone has a weight and leans over to the side, they are doing a Leaning Tower of Pisa.

An older man had been working out at a club for several months, and one day his wife decided to try going to the club. Being she was parked behind his car, she would drive them to the club. She wrote down the combination for her locker so she wouldn't forget the combination and put it in her pocket. Then she looked for a trainer to show her what machines to use. Later a couple of ladies waved at her, and for the life of her she couldn't remember where she had seen them. Finally, after an hour, she had had enough and was getting ready to leave. Gathering up all her equipment and hoping she had remembered everything, she went home. Not more than a half-hour after getting home, her husband called and said, "Did you forget something?"

Work Situations

Your boss stands outside the office door, timing when you come in, and says, "At least you're only twenty minutes late instead of your usual thirty."

Your boss looks at you and says, "You look good today. The way you looked the other day, you looked rather sick."

Looking at your new hairdo, the manager says, "I don't know what they did to your hair, but I am sure we can find someone who can try to fix it."

"Jorge, you got it right; there is a first time for everything."

"I know this meeting is about people stealing other people's ideas. Larry, you don't need to be here; you haven't had any ideas in years."

Boss to employee: "I know you need more water than most people because you are always hanging out at the water cooler, so I have decided to move it next to your desk so you won't even need to get up."

"You are dressing better. Your clothes no longer look they came from Goodwill but from a discount store."

Boss to employee: "I know how you like to think and daydream a lot, so I am going to give you some time off to do that."

Employee complaining to boss: "Every Christmas for the past three years at our Christmas exchange, I get a bar of soap and everyone who works around me gets a strong cologne. Well, the smell is getting to me."

You see those who work with you don't take your ideas seriously. "I will take care of it." When he leaves, the boss tells his secretary, "Tell Jim mad Sue, good work for overlooking his dumb ideas."

"You know, Willie is our worst worker, lazy, not too bright, and gets little done. Now you have been here six months and you are starting to make Willie look good."

A lady said her husband was a gem. He was a janitor who sweated her off her feet. He promised to clean up her messes and best of all. he promised a clean bathroom.

Another lady said her husband was pretty good, too. He was a detective who was always dusting for fingerprints, and when everything was lost he was good at looking for clues and solving the mystery where it was. He was also great at booking things if you wanted to go anywhere.

A happy tool man is just tooling along.

First words of a carpenter's son: "I saw."

Eye doctor teaching his son to learn the alphabet: "Cover your eye, now read the eye chart."

A Photographer:
I feel like I have only one good shot at being a success.
I tell people I will be back in a flash.
I say there is a developing story and in a hour there will be pictures.
I hope to expose what is happening.

A date with an undertaker:
He said, "I hope you don't mind me taking the hearse; my car is in the shop."
He gave me beautiful flowers. I didn't ask, "From whose funeral?"
Before we ate, he took out a makeup kit and helped me with my makeup. He knows how to make people look good.
While we ate, he entertained me with stories of secrets that people took with them to the grave.
He said he believed in leaving the past behind and not digging it up again.
He also said he didn't like to throw dirt at anyone.
He claimed he was well grounded.
He offered me some discount coupons if I were to need them.
We then went for a drive so we could pick up a body to bring back to the funeral home.
I hoped I would never get in a hole deep enough to have to date him again.

Index